Revenge of the Pylon Bird

by David Horne

Credits

Illustrations by Polly Hastilow
Cover photograph by Paul Goodrick
Maps and Broad Oak Lakes photograph by David Horne

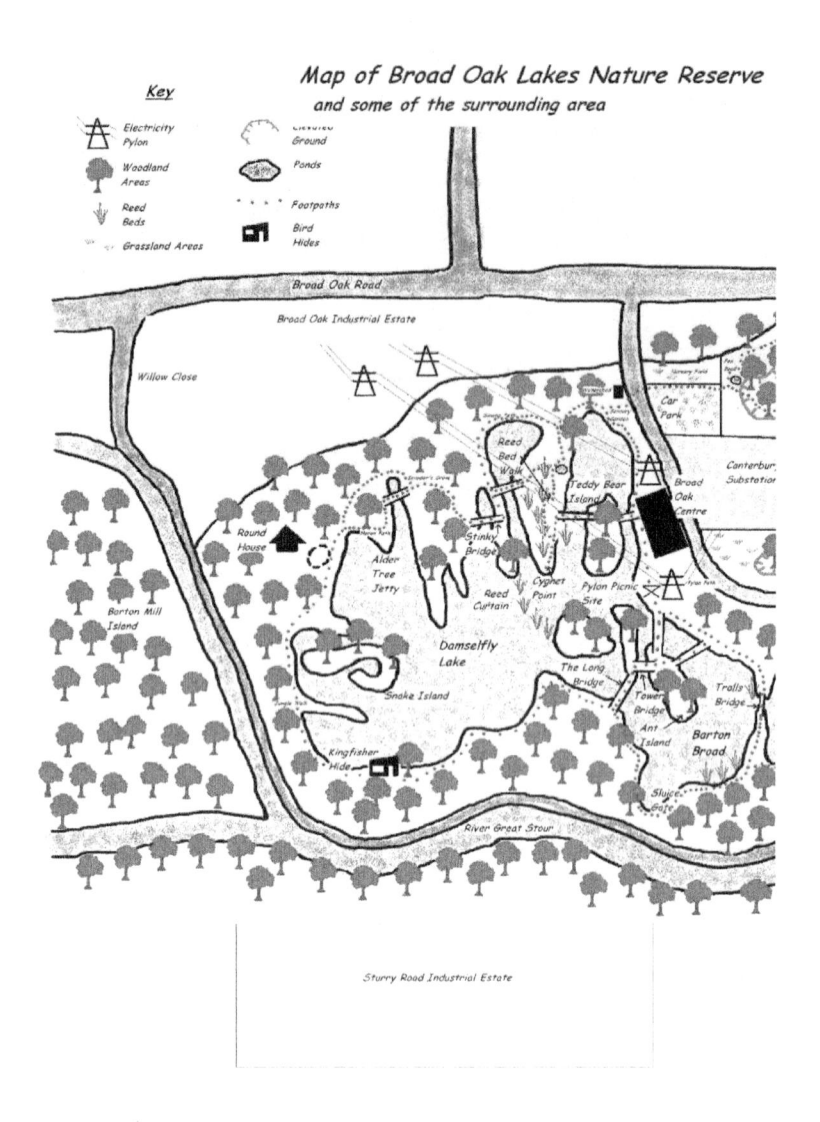

Map of Broad Oak Lakes Nature Reserve
and some of the surrounding area

Key
- Electricity Pylon
- Woodland Areas
- Reed Beds
- Grassland Areas
- Elevated Ground
- Ponds
- Footpaths
- Bird Hides

Broad Oak Road

Broad Oak Industrial Estate

Willow Close

Car Park

Reed Bed Walk

Teddy Bear Island

Broad Oak Centre

Canterbury Substation

Round House

Alder Tree Jetty

Stinky Bridge

Cygnet Point

Reed Curtain

Pylon Picnic Site

Barton Mill Island

Damselfly Lake

The Long Bridge

Snake Island

Tower Bridge

Trolls Bridge

Ant Island

Barton Broad

Kingfisher Hide

Sluice Gate

River Great Stour

Sturry Road Industrial Estate

(west side)

Map of Broad Oak Lakes Nature Reserve
and some of the surrounding area

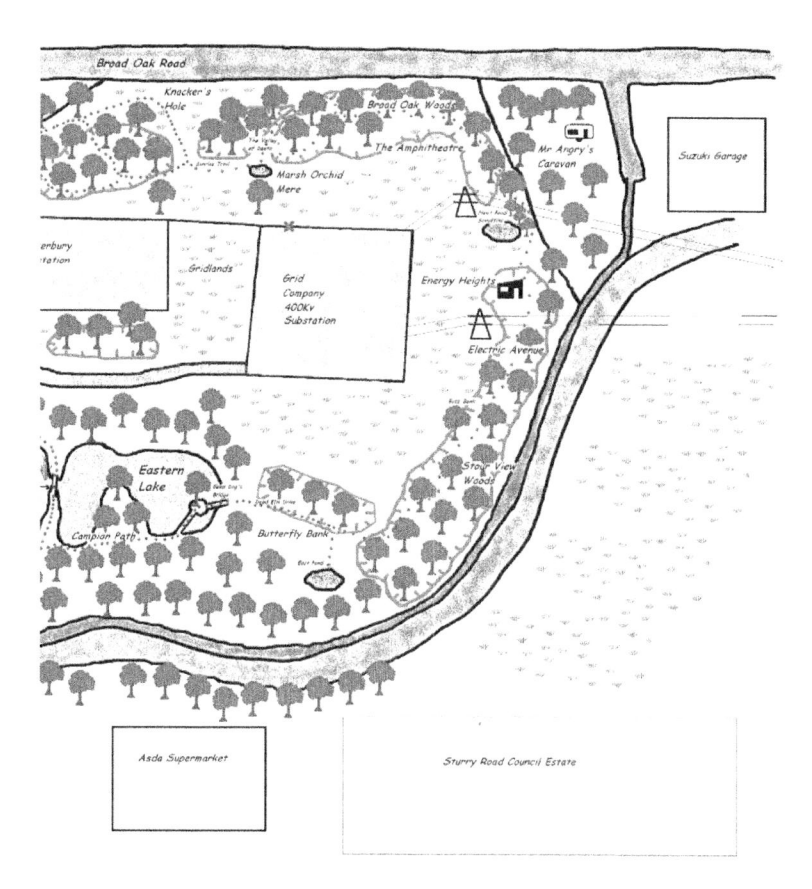

(east side)

Chapter One
The Secret Agent

'Here they come!' a voice called out.

'Fat old git in a Jag is coming' added another.

As the motorcade accompanying the government minister approached, complete with police outriders on their gleaming motorcycles, the gathered crowd of protesters started to jeer and cat-call.

One of the protesters, his face obscured from the watching TV cameras by a motorcycle helmet and the positioning of a young police constable standing directly in front of him, was not joining in. No sound or gesture of protest came from him. Dressed totally in black leather and black helmet he stood aloof amongst the chanting and jeering crowd. As the group of black ministerial cars and police motorcyclists came into view he tensed in anticipation, the adrenalin rushing through his bloodstream causing his body to almost scream for action. After years of practice though, he knew how to control it, waiting for his moment.

Then as the minister's car approached, he bursts out

of the crowd, pushing over the young policeman in front of him. In his hand he carried a small package. It was his intention to share its contents with the unsuspecting senior politician sitting smug and safe in his bullet-proof, chauffer-driven Jaguar. As he approached the car, the nearest police outrider saw him and changed direction to head him off. The second police motorcyclist, a few meters behind, accelerated to assist his colleague. The young policeman, now lying prostrate in the gutter, picked himself up and set off after his assailant. As the three officers closed in on him, the helmeted interloper drew his arm back and threw the package full force at the windscreen of the car.

As the missile closed on its target he thought to himself, every TV screen in the country would carry the news of what he had done today, in the name of animal rights. Next moment he felt the jolt he had been expecting, as the young policeman rugby tackled him from behind. Nonetheless, his moment of fame was now guaranteed as the package exploded onto the cars windscreen.

'Very theatrical' said the anonymous voice from the darkened corner of the interrogation room at Canterbury Police Station. 'You certainly got the nation's attention, with that stunt. Old Preston probably 'peed' his pants when the ink exploded on his windscreen'.

'Well all in a day's work I suppose' replied Smith 'There are a few perks to be gained from this job you know? By the way who brought me down, he should get a trial for the Lion's rugby team with a tackle like that?'

'He probably will some day. He's already played for England Under 21's'. Smith could almost see the grin on Cyclop's face as he revealed this fact.

'I might have guessed. There's always got to be some angle that doesn't work out in these operations'

'True, but just think what you've done for his career, it must be one of the most televised rugby tackles in history! The tabloid papers will be full of 'young police constable foils terrorist attack'. Biggest problem for us will be keeping the 'terrorist's identity from the media. Still, hopefully the publicity will improve your stock with your wacky animal-loving chums'

Smith was in fact an undercover operative for the secret government organization which referred to itself as 'The Squad'. Smith and his colleagues, none of whom he had ever come into contact with, were given the task of infiltrating terrorist organizations and supplying information to the 'official' security organizations.

His only contact was his handler who went by the name of Cyclops, the one eyed monster from Greek Mythology. The first time they met, was in a darkened room (In fact come to think of it they always seemed to meet in darkened rooms). During the whole meeting Cyclops wore dark glasses. However, when code names were discussed, it wasn't the one eyed Greek monster that Smith was thinking of when he gave the name Cyclops to his handler, but the superhero from the Sci-Fi film 'The 'X' Men' - the one who never took his dark glasses off, for fear of blasting people with his laser vision. The other man had laughed understandingly. In return he had given

Smith his name, betraying his knowledge of science fiction films. Smith wasn't keen on being likened to the villain in the Matrix, but at least the name was more anonymous than Anderson or Neo.

Smith did have another name, but when he was on squad business he erased it from his mind (Anyway if he were to reveal his true identity he would have to kill you and that would rather spoil the point of telling this story).

Smith's specialty was animal rights terrorists.

'So what's new?' said Smith a little cockily. 'I know all about the increased animal rights activity in East Kent. But are we any nearer to breaking the East Kent cell?'

'You will be aware that over the last few years, members of the Animal Liberation Front (ALF) have been conducting a campaign of terror against companies linked to Huntingdon Life Sciences (HLS) near Cambridge.' Began Cyclops.

'This terrorism has included attacks on directors and employees of the company, as well as action against people more distantly linked to it.' He continued.

'Like the case involving attacks on the farm that breeds guinea pigs for experimental work carried out by HLS.' Added Smith.

'Quite' Said Cyclops, tucking in his chin and tilting his nose downwards so that he could glare at Smith over the top of his dark glasses. His sharp tone betrayed his irritation at being interrupted. 'The extremists even dug up the grave of one of the owners late relatives!'

'Your job,' continued Cyclops, 'is to infiltrate the East Kent cell of ALF and discover what they might be planning. As you know, we suspect their main target is likely to be the animal research laboratories at the university science park.'

'Well that's why me and my animal protest chums have been making so much noise there over the past few months.' Smiled Smith, who had often been one of these demonstrators. Although he had always taken care to conceal his features inside a motorcycle helmet.

'Well it seems likely that the East Kent cell, is about to carry out a more threatening campaign of violence.' Said Cyclops. 'And as always, terrorism attracts the maximum of publicity. So our guess is they will probably attack the laboratories head on.'

'And my job is to determine when and how they plan to do this and then tip off your lot. Is that right?' Said Smith.

Smith had not been able to find out who the real hard-core animal activists were, despite being familiar with many of the less antisocial protesters. Some of these were young and dread-locked, moving between animal activism, Greenpeace protests and other organizations of conscience, such as Amnesty International. They were young, principled idealists, still searching for their place in the world.

In total contrast others were little old ladies supporting

a house full of cats, to which they had already willed their considerable wealth.

Other protesters were young couples with children, whom they dragged along with them to protests; often looking a little bewildered like the children of those religious sects you may experience spreading their beliefs on the doorsteps of reluctant suburban homeowners.

'Have you any idea which of that mixed-bag of characters who had lined up in protest at the gates of North Downs Life Sciences might be the hard-core activists?' Questioned Cyclops. 'The one's prepared to go to any length to stop the use of animals in the interests of medical research?'

Smith had his own views on the treatment of animals, but he had no time for this bunch, their twisted morals and the extreme lengths they were prepared to go to, often threatening the lives of innocent members of the public.

'Possibly.' Added Smith. 'My hunch is it has to be someone connected with money, lots of it. There is one obvious person that comes to mind. You know who I mean of course. So what happens next?'

'Well hopefully, after your theatrical performance today, you'll now find it easier to infiltrate their ring so that we can nail them. My guess is that they will try to knock out the laboratories' main power source.' Confided Cyclops. 'I have a suspicion that they will look to find some way to cut this supply off'.

'How are you proposing protecting this supply? Asked

Smith.

'That's where the problem lies.' Said Cyclops 'We carried out a review of their security and we found a problem, their power supply needs a major rethink. We have recommended they get a much more secure system, but this will take several months. In the meantime they will continue to get their power direct from the substation at Broad Oak Lakes, which also supplies power to the whole of the Canterbury area.'

'I can see where you are going with this' Added Smith 'Knowing the mentality of those involved you think they might carry out some sort of attack at Broad Oak Lakes. They would have no problem cutting off the whole of the East Kent power supply at the same time.'

'Yes and that would lead to all sorts of problems, including power loss to hospitals, schools, people's houses and local industry' Said Cyclops.

'So what are you doing about it?' asked Smith.

'We already have it under low level surveillance' confided Cyclops 'You know 'One Man and his Dog' watching out, carefully hidden amongst the dense woodland cover of the surrounding nature reserve. However, what I want is for you to get close also, using whatever guise you choose.'
'You mean you want me to find some way of getting more information about the comings and goings of anyone who might show an interest in the place' Said Smith.

'Naturally' said Cyclops 'All the SAS Men in the world,

and their dogs, can't get the sort of information we need, just by standing guard. Anyway we want to catch these people in the act, so that we can destroy their organization. No you have to use one of your many aliases to give you an excuse to visit the site. The nature reserve attracts all sorts of people with legitimate business interests. I am sure they will greet you with open arms, if you indicate that you can put some form of income their way.'

'OK, I shouldn't have any problems there, in fact I've got a few ideas already' said Smith.

'Good' Chuckled Cyclops 'I never for a moment expected otherwise.'

'I'll have to have a clear field though,' Explained Smith, 'which means you'll have to stop your surveillance activities once I'm in place. If we want to break the whole ring we don't want to risk your man and his dog blowing the whole cover'

'OK. Let me know when you are ready and I'll make him disappear. In the meantime I suggest you slip out through the canteen fire exit, unless you want to have your identity plastered all over the papers.' Cyclops gave a wry grin as he made the suggestion.

'No thanks' said Smith 'How're you going to keep me a secret?'

'No problem, leave that to us. Now go' said Cyclops with an air of finality.

Taking his cue, Smith got up, left the interrogation room and as arranged slipped quietly out of the back exit, melting anonymously into the crowds of French tourists swarming towards Canterbury Cathedral. Immediately, he became one of them, just another person with a particular interest in Canterbury. However, his interests were about to take him a mile downstream to the Broad Oak Lakes Nature Reserve.

He had to get to the bottom of what was going on, with regard to the very real threat posed by this particular group of fanatics. So far he had had no success through his animal rights activities. Maybe he'd do better if he concentrated on the substation.

Chapter Two

Shoot-out at the Grove

'Zing - crack'. A wood pigeon burst out from the branches of the leafless tree above, scattering a few dead winter twigs as it went. But it was not the pigeon that had made the noise. Ben ducked down, his arms covering his head involuntarily, his whole body shaking with expectation. Next to him Joe was lying similarly prostrate on the woodland floor, a look of fear in his eyes.

'Someone is shooting at us.' Wailed the eleven year old 'I think someone's trying to kill us.'

'No they're not' said Ben reassuringly. Although he was nearly thirteen, he wasn't going to show his own fear to his younger friend. 'I think it's someone trying to shoot birds. Probably someone from the travelers' encampment'

Ben hoped he sounded confident, more confident than he actually felt. As if to prove his point he stood up and looked around him. Almost immediately there was another crack and Ben flinched, but he realized the shot was some distance away and that he had guessed right. The marksman was now no longer a threat.

Ben took a couple of steps in the direction of the shooting.

'What you doing?' Exclaimed Joe, in some alarm.

'I'm going to have a look and see who's shooting' Replied Ben 'Come on.'

Keeping a few paces behind his older and bolder friend, Joe followed. The two boys made their way at a crouching run towards the edge of the wood, whilst at the same time tingling with both fear and excitement. When they reached the woodland edge they were able to see the open field beyond, separating the wood from the encroaching housing estate, on the edge of Felixstowe.
Off to their left, about a hundred metres away, they could see two lads, both probably in their late teens. One of them had an air-rifle under his arm and was in the process of reloading it. Both were dressed in regulation blue jeans, 'hoodies' and baseball caps. The one holding the air-rifle wore a red 'hoodie', whilst his mate's was dark blue. The latter was busily gesticulating towards the woods, apparently instructing his friend about where to shoot.

Ben didn't like people who were mean to animals, but he was especially protective of the animals of The Grove, as he regarded them as being his own and these two were invading his territory.

Feeling a bit more confident about the situation, now

that he could see his adversaries and they could not see him, Ben said 'Let's get a bit closer and see what they are up to'.

Joe was not so keen on this idea but didn't want to appear frightened in front of his older friend. Somewhat nervously, both boys made their way along the edge of the wood, the naked January trees providing sufficient cover to give them confidence that they could not be seen by the 'enemy'. They had played games of 'commandoes' many times before in these woods, but this was somehow different, there was a real 'enemy' to stalk. Ben could feel the combination of excitement and fear running up and down his spine, making his hand tremble and his throat dry as they picked their way amongst the trees.

Crawling on their stomachs to avoid detection and shielded by the woodland bank that encircled The Grove, they were now within 50 metres of the two lads and close enough to hear the conversation in the field beyond in the still January air.

'Come on Jed you can do better than that. If I can hit a robin at 50 yards, you should be able to hit that bloody great pigeon' Said the one in the blue 'hoodie'.

Jed was obviously stung by this comment and steadied himself to take careful aim at his quarry. Just as he was about to pull the trigger and potentially dispatch the unfortunate animal to an early grave, Joe's mobile phone went off. It was only the alarm bell ring tone, reminding him that he was due home for tea in 15 minutes, but it was enough to put the marksman off his shot.

'Missed - you stupid dip' laughed the one in blue.

'Oy! Who's that?' said Jed, gesticulating in the direction of the noise. 'Someone's out there Shane!'

'Where? You pulling my leg?' Accused his mate

'Didn't you hear it? Someone's phone went off!'

'Yeah! Any excuse'

'I'm not joking. There's someone over there watching us' said Jed, pointing directly at where Ben and Joe lay concealed.

'You sure?'

'Course'

'All right let's have a look then. But this'd better not be another of your lousy excuses! Crap-shot Kid'. He taunted him.

The two young boys hiding at the edge of the woodland froze, wondering what to do next. The two older lads were headed in their direction and would see them in just a few seconds. What should they do?

'Come on' Whispered Ben, turning and crawling quickly away into the deeper cover of the woodland. Within a few seconds he was safely concealed behind an elder shrub, its pale green winter foliage still clinging tightly to its branches and offering some degree of protection. It was only then that he realized that Joe had not followed, but was still frozen to the spot at the edge of the woods, his eyes closed and his hands over his head in the hope that no-one would see him.

'There he is' said Jed, pointing at Joe's ill concealed body. 'Bleedin' spy. Put me off mi shot. Get up you little shit' He barked at Joe.

The eleven year old stood up, terrified. His face ashen.

'What you going to do Jed?' Said Shane, anticipating the sport to come.

'I'm going to pulverize the little bugger.' Said Jed, grabbing hold of Joe by the collar.

'Leave him alone' Shouted Ben, stepping out of the cover of the elder shrub, his blood starting to rise at the prospect of these two bullies threatening his friend.

'It's against the law to shoot at birds, I'll call the police.' He threatened unconvincingly.

'There's another one.' Cackled Shane. 'This one's going to grass on us. What you going to do about it Jed?'

'Come here!' Commanded Jed, pointing his outstretched finger at Ben, 'Or I'll give your friend here a good thumping!'

Reluctant to do as the older boy commanded, but also terrified of the consequences of not doing, Ben took a couple of hesitant steps forwards.

'What are you going to do to us?' Cried Joe, now visibly shaking with fear.

'It's OK Joe' Reassured Ben.

'No it's not OK' Contradicted Jed, the anger showing clearly on his face as he took the few steps between him and Ben, grabbing him by the collar. Jed had obviously lost all self control by now and was intent on taking his frustration out on Ben. Like all bullies, he blamed all his own failings on someone smaller and weaker than himself. Being a bad shot and failing to hit a bird, unlike his friend Shane, was patently not his fault. It was Ben's.

'Leave me alone' Shouted Ben, struggling to free himself from the much bigger lad.

But instead of letting him go, Jed swung Ben around and threw him to the ground at Shane's feet. This was looking serious, as Jed became more and more worked up with Ben. Ben was now really scared, realizing that the out-of-control Jed was capable of almost anything.

Then his mate suddenly interjected 'Look out it's that wildlife warden coming up the field. Come on, next thing you know he'll have the cops on us for shooting at birds.'

Shane dropped the body of the dead robin he had shot earlier, at Ben's feet, turned tail and bolted off into the woods.

'Come on.' He urged his friend. 'Leave them.' And he disappeared from view.

Jed hesitated for a second, but his own cowardice and fear quickly displaced his anger and he too ran off into the woods.

'I'll have you next time I see you,' Jed shouted back at Ben threateningly. Then he was gone, leaving the two badly shaken boys alone, staring at each other. Ben felt close to tears, whilst Joe couldn't hold his emotions in any longer and wept openly.

Ben bent down and picked up the lifeless body of the robin. A small amount of blood marked the point of entry of the air gun pellet, barely visible against its crimson coloured breast.

'I suppose we were lucky' lamented Ben, showing the carcass to his younger friend, who stopped crying as Ben held the little form cupped in his hands. 'This little chap wasn't so fortunate.'

'What you got there then you little scally-wags' Came a deep resonant voice behind them.

Ben looked up startled by the newcomer, a large, thick set man in his late fifties, wearing a flat cap and a bright green sweatshirt with the name and logo of the local wildlife trust emblazoned on it.
'It's an offence to shoot at birds you know. Did you kill the poor little beast? I'm going to have to report this to the police. You'd better come with me young fellers.'

****

The police officer who turned up ten minutes later,

took Ben and Joe's names and addresses as a matter of course, but reassured them, after they had explained their story, that they were not in trouble. He took the descriptions of Jed and Shane and complimented Ben on the detailed nature of his observations. He also offered them both a word of advice.

'If ever you find yourself in a similar situation, report the matter straight to the police and don't play at being spies. Leave it to us in future.'

It was sound advice that Ben would consider on a couple of occasions over the coming months, but with markedly different outcomes.

'OK, you young heroes, how do you fancy a lift home?' Offered the police officer. This rather cheered Joe up after the ordeal of being shot at, threatened by thugs, caught by a nature reserve warden and cautioned by a policeman.
He dropped Ben off first, who waved goodbye to a delighted Joe as he grinned from the back seat of the police car.

As Ben opened the door he wondered whether to tell his parents about the incident. He didn't want to worry them, particularly his mum. Both his parents had been a bit tense of late, ever since his dad had been made redundant at work.

Still undecided about whether to mention his scrape, he walked into the living room, where his mum, dad and sister Beth were chatting excitedly.

Before he could ask what all the excitement was

about, his father jumped up, with a big grin on his face.

'We're moving to Kent' Dad announced.

'Yes, he's got a great new job in Canterbury' Mum chipped in, with an approving smile on her face. 'He's going to run the nature reserve there'.

'Isn't that super' said Beth full of the enthusiasm you would expect from a 5 year old.

Ben said nothing. He just sat there staring ahead of him thinking black thoughts.

'Got nothing to say Ben?' Chirped Dad

'Great' said Ben, but his heart said 'Oh no, another move, here we go again'

Chapter Three
Grey Beginnings

The grey February drizzle fell out of the drab, overcast sky as Ben sat in the old wooden bird hide staring at the grey pylons, wires and other machinery that made up the electricity substation. It seemed as though the whole world had turned grey. What kind of a place was this? The wires overhead hummed and crackled as the drops of rainwater vapourised on contact with the 400,000 volts of electricity that ran from the substation on their never-ending circuit of the country.

Even the North Sea at Felixstowe was not as grey and lifeless as this, he thought. Beyond the substation the nature reserve was also a dull, grey-brown colour. Leafless trees peered through the murk. A hammering sound drifted on the wind, coming from the industrial area beyond the river. He couldn't for the life of him see what made Dad so excited about working in a place like this. He just sat and stared for several minutes at the unchanging landscape ahead of him, wishing he were back home playing with his mate Joe.

'Hi' said a girl's voice from behind him. So unexpected

was this that he physically leapt into the air making the newcomer giggle. Embarrassed by his reaction and a little annoyed by the interloper's unexpected appearance, his face reddened and his brow furrowed.

'Who are you?' he asked rather rudely.

'Pleased to meet you too!' said the girl, who was a similar age to him, but annoyingly an inch or two taller. He didn't like girls much at the best of times and he was just a bit afraid of girls who were taller than him, although he would never admit it.

When she failed to get the apology she was anticipating, the girl pressed on.

'My name's Elizabeth. Lizzie Trowbridge. What's yours?'

'What?' he muttered, taken aback by her forthright attitude. 'What are you doing here? It's private property you know?'

The girl stiffened 'Oh is it? Well I'd better go before you have me arrested hadn't I?' And she turned to leave.

'Sorry' He apologized, realizing his rudeness 'You made me jump that's all. I was just looking at the substation and the rain and you surprised me'

'Well that's all-right then. As I was saying, my name's Lizzie and I live in the house on the main road over there' Pointing off to her right. 'So do you have a name?'

She seemed to have no fear at all, standing there with her short curly hair, dressed in denim jeans and one of those black hooded jackets, edged with black fur, that all girls of her age seemed to wear. He could see that it wasn't particularly waterproof, by the dark, rain-soaked patches on her shoulders. This made him feel a bit easier, thinking to himself that she wasn't so clever after all. On the other hand, he was wearing one of those heavy green really waterproof cagoules that his Mum insisted he wear at the first sign of rain.

'Ben. My name's Ben Franklin. My Dad is the boss here'. He said, gesturing towards the nature reserve and trying to sound a little superior. However Lizzie didn't seem to show any reaction to this statement.

'You've just moved here then have you? I thought I'd not seen you before.' Making herself comfortable she sat on the bench next to him, too close for a 13 year old boy's comfort. He shuffled slightly away from her. He nodded, mumbling something about Felixstowe under his breath.

'Well I hope your Dad doesn't mind me sheltering from the rain for a few minutes? Do you like it here? I think it's great just walking round here on my own, although it's a bit grim at this time of year in this weather' pointing at the grey world beyond.

Ben was surprised by her enthusiasm for the place. 'Can't see that there's anything special about it' he said 'just a few trees around a power station'

'Substation.' She corrected him 'It's an electricity substation. They don't make the electricity here, they just change it to a voltage suited to factories and houses in the area'.

'Oh?' said Ben, once again on the back foot as a result of her superior knowledge. 'Yes my dad works as substation manager, so he explained it to me. All those bits of wire and things are pretty weird and they all do different things. Mind you, if you touched one there wouldn't be much left of you!'

Even from within the bird hide the high voltage humming was evident, emanating from the massive 400,000 volt transformers and their protective blast walls.

Lizzie pointed towards them saying 'My dad told me that the walls are there to protect the rest of the compound in case the transformers have a problem and explode unexpectedly.'

'Blimey, I hope they don't explode today.'

"Don't worry,' she reassured him, 'you are more likely to be hit by lightening'

'I don't fancy that either thanks' laughed Ben.

Ben found himself warming to her a little, her openness helping him to relax, as she went into some detail about the substation and how it worked.

'But your Dad's got a much better job than mine. What happens in there', she said pointing towards the substation, 'is boring compared to the nature reserve around it'

As if to prove her wrong Ben caught sight of a movement within the compound, next to one of the access holes leading to the underground cable ducts.

'Look' said Ben 'one of those foxes that use the underground passageways for shelter during the winter-time, I think they must snuggling up against the insulated high voltage cables, to keep warm.'

'Oh I see it' said Lizzie, 'It may be the fox I saw a few days ago, at Pylon Picnic Site, with a moorhen in its mouth.'

As they now watched they could see the fox's head as it peered out of its den. It was a fairly small individual and seemed a bit scrawny, its rather tatty coat showing all the hallmarks of the mange that many foxes seem to suffer from.

Satisfied that nobody was watching, the fox scampered out of its hole, through the compound fence and headed up towards Electric Avenue, probably intent on hunting for further hapless waterfowl along the river bank, or perhaps heading off towards the local land-fill site to scavenge for bits of rotting food waste, unwittingly donated by Canterbury householders.

'There it goes' whispered Ben, as it trotted up the slope. Suddenly a large animal shot out from the undergrowth in the direction of the fox. It was a large German Shepherd Dog, its ears pricked and eyes focused on its red-coated cousin.

The fox, ever alert to danger, immediately spotted the threatening charge of the dog and veered off left towards the bird hide at Energy Heights. The nature reserve's top carnivore suddenly found itself to be the quarry of a much bigger predator, apparently intent on turning the fox into lunch. The fox broke into a gallop as the dog closed in on it. To Ben it was obvious that the fox was the slower of the two, especially considering the down-slope momentum the big dog had in its favour.

However, both Ben and the dog had failed to reckon with the natural guile of the fox. Just as the dog was about to sink its teeth into the foxes smooth rufus pelt, the fox jinked sideways into a narrow passageway in a bramble thicket, leaving the surprised dog with jaws full of fresh air. A fraction of a second later the dog gave an alarmed yelp as it tumbled headlong into the brambles.

The fox emerged from the other side of the thicket and cantered up the hill to the ridge. As it topped the rise it paused momentarily to look back in the direction of its scratched and thwarted assailant. Satisfied that the danger had passed, the fox turned and with its white tipped bushy tail extended nonchalantly behind it, it made off into the trees beyond.

Suddenly there came a shrill whistle from the direction in which the dog had first appeared. The dog turned and trotted back towards the whistler. As it reached the thick cover provided by the trees and bushes on top of the hill, a tall black clad figure, with a droopy moustache stepped out to meet it.

From their hill-top view Ben and Lizzie had a fleeting view of something slung over the man's shoulder. To his surprise Ben realized that the man was carrying a powerful automatic rifle, similar to the ones carried by policemen he had seen at Heathrow Airport and by soldiers at the entrance to the barracks in Canterbury.

The armed policeman attached a leash to the dog's collar, whilst the dog sat obediently at his feet, then the two of them turned-tail back into the cover of the trees and disappeared.

'Did you see that?' Gaped Lizzie. 'That looked like a machine gun he was carrying.'

They just looked at each other dumb-founded, both thinking. 'What could such a heavily armed policeman and his highly trained dog be doing hiding in the trees of a nature-reserve?'

****

From his vantage point amongst the tree cover of Buzz Bank, the shadowy individual observed the movements of the boy and girl as each had entered the bird hide, nestled in the wooded area directly opposite him. It was the first opportunity he had taken to survey the site.

He noted that the two large substations occupied open ground surrounded by a ring of low, tree-capped, man-made hills designed to conceal the mass of complex electrical structures from the surrounding factories and houses. The larger of the two substations was surrounded by an electrified fence and some 20 or 30 metres of open ground. The surrounding woodland provided reasonable cover for surveillance work.

Through his binoculars he had been able to see the two children talking in the hide and noticed them pointing excitedly at something inside the compound. He had then shared their view of the confrontation between the fox and the police dog. He was not impressed.

Cyclops had told him about the police presence on site. It was now evident that if they were going to snare the animal activists, covert surveillance was not going to be the way.

Smith realized that his best way of keeping an eye on the substation was going to require him to come out from the trees and to either find a way of working at the nature reserve, or blend in with the many other characters who came and went across the site. He was going to have to use all his trade-craft and create himself an identity that would give him free and open access to the site. He knew exactly how to do that.

Chapter Four
Creamer of City Hall

As February turned to March all Lizzie's predictions about springtime on the nature reserve proved to be true. As Ben walked around the lakes he would discover something new every day. First to appear were the snowdrops pushing their heads up through the fallen leaves of autumn in Canterbury Woods.

He and Lizzie would sometimes sit on the end of Snake Island in the early morning mist, in the hope of seeing a kingfisher or even one of the otter's that rumour had it came up the river. That they never saw them made little difference to the pleasure of exploring this world that no-one else was aware of. Ben liked Lizzie, especially the unembarrassed way in which she chattered about almost anything, wildlife, people, electricity, the history of the area. She was a mine of information, but never used it to show off.

One day as he sat alone in the Kingfisher Hide watching the mallards and tufted ducks maneuvering around on the lake, like fleets of ships preparing to give each other a broadside, he heard a familiar voice outside. It was his father. A second voice could be heard, higher pitched, lacking any obvious accent, in sharp contrast to his father's, much deeper voice with its distinct Yorkshire tones.

As they paused by the door to the bird-hide he could hear his father rattling off all sorts of facts and figures about wildlife and his work. As always when he got on a 'roll', his voice would get louder and he would become animated, getting excited about the activities that visiting school children carried out.

The other man was obviously someone fairly senior being given a guided tour in the hope of making a good impression. However, there was something about his tone and the style of questioning that made Ben instantly dislike the man. He sounded more interested in costs and the number of employees rather than reacting favourably to his father's enthusiasm for the environment and children's learning opportunities. Ben had never come across someone who so obviously failed to be drawn in by his father's infectious enthusiasm. Ben often found it embarrassing when he got up on his 'hobby horse', but everyone seemed to delight in the stories and excitement he generated. Not this character, with his flat toned voice and air of superiority.

Then the door burst open and his father came in, stopping suddenly when he saw Ben.

'Well what do we have here, a pirate perhaps or a spy? What do you think we should do with him Mr. Creamer?' he said turning to his guest.

Ben grinned at his father, a man of 50 but a boy of 10. The other man stood a few feet behind his father, looking a little awkward and obviously incapable of contributing towards his father's banter. Mr. Creamer's long thin face, topped by a head of thin, mouse-coloured, straight hair showed little sign of a smile. He managed a slight upturn to the corners of his mouth, but his eyes did not betray one iota of good humour. Ben felt himself shiver as the man entered the bird hide.

'This is my son Ben', proclaimed his father.

'Hello young man. Not at school today? I suppose a young scallywag like you prefers to be hiding away instead of getting his head down to some serious work?' As the man got closer Ben caught a whiff of cigarette smoke on the man's clothes. His yellowing teeth and the nicotine stains on his fingers further gave away his habit.

'Easter Holiday.' Chipped in his father, shooting Ben a look that said it all. His father's eyes rolled, whilst the right hand side of his top lip curled upwards. Ben had to look down at the ground in an effort to stop himself giggling at his father's reaction to Creamer.

'Ah, I see' said Creamer, realizing that perhaps he was the butt of a father and son joke. Then he turned his irritation onto the rustic building they were standing in.

'A bit rough and ready, but I suppose it serves its purpose. Personally I can't see the attraction of sitting in a draughty shed waiting for a pigeon or something to find the time to appear. Still I suppose there must be some people who enjoy it'

'It was built by volunteers and is very popular with visitors as a place to pause and enjoy the views across the lake.' Said his father, perhaps a touch too defensively. 'The only cost to the council was the wood, most of which was recycled from a previous bird hide'

'Yes I can see that.' Said Creamer, a little patronizingly, 'But it doesn't really represent the quality of workmanship that the council would want to be associated with.'

'I think it's great' contributed Ben 'Kids love places like this. It makes me feel like some sort of explorer or pioneer in the Wild West'

His Dad smiled at him and roughed his hair up, whilst all Creamer could manage was raised eyebrows and pursed lips.

'Well I suppose we ought to be getting along. I need to be back at the office by three and I still need to go over those financial projections of yours' Said Creamer, as he turned on his heels and stepped out of the door, only to put his foot into a large pile of green slimy swan pooh thoughtfully left by Sebastian or Sarah, the reserve's resident swans.

The green slime covered his shiny black shoes, peppering the trouser bottoms of his sharp grey suit. The look of disgust and a slow, theatrical expulsion of breath said it all as he looked meaningfully at Ben's father, before turning and marching off with Dad in hot pursuit.

This was to be Ben's first but by no means his last encounter with Mr. Creamer.

****

'Do you know what that toad Creamer said to me today?' Asked Dad. He had just returned home, where Ben, his mum and his sister had just sat down to their evening meal. 'The Education Committee has taken the decision to withdraw our subsidy and unless we can raise enough funding from other sources by September 1st, none of us will have jobs come next April.'

'But they've only just taken you on' Said Mum with obvious alarm 'How could they drag us all the way down here, only to threaten to throw us all out a year later? Who are these people?'

'I know. Doesn't he realize that means we have got to double our income over the next five months?' Continued Dad, pacing up and down the dining room carpet like a Coldstream guard on duty outside Buckingham Palace.

Dad did not often get worked up into such a 'lather' but when he did, Ben knew it was a good idea to keep a low profile and just let him talk, uninterrupted.

We'll have to make savings. I'm afraid I may have to let old Charlie go as well.'

'But he's been working at Broad Oak Lakes for years. It's his life' Thought Ben, not daring to say it out loud.

'I know what you're thinking, but what can I do? If you can find a crock of gold buried on the reserve, or better still find a way to get Creamer to change his mind, then that's the kind of miracle we are now praying for.'

'I think I'll have a look at those figures again and see where we might make cuts or raise more money.' Then shoulders noticeably slumped, he walked out of the room leaving his untouched food to go cold on its plate.

Chapter Five
An Encounter with Mr. Angry

What better place in the world could there be than Butterfly Bank on a sunny Sunday afternoon in May? Ben lay stretched out on the grass, the warm sun on his face, listening for any sounds around him. No noise from the surrounding industrial estates, just the sound of blackbirds, willow warblers, wrens and robins singing love songs to potential mates.

Butterfly Bank was a natural sun-trap. No wind seemed to penetrate the glade here, surrounded by trees and separating Ben's own little world from the real world beyond.

Sunday afternoon at Broad Oak Lakes, the world beyond might as well not exist. Just the sound of the gentlest of breezes in the trees, causing them to whisper to each other about the latest antics of the dog fox or when they might expect the first cuckoo to appear. A humming sound in his right ear told him that the bees, wasps and hoverflies were busy.

He had been lying there for some 30 minutes, dozing in the first warmth of the fledgling summer, thinking about nothing in particular, when he heard a distant cry disturb the tranquility of the day. He sat up and listened, trying to work out where it was coming from. If it was across the river, beyond the trees, then it was probably one of the 'yobs' from the estate throwing stones at one of the beleaguered moorhens that hid in the waters-edge vegetation. He hated those kids and what they did to the unfortunate wildlife across the river and felt a twinge of anger at the thought of one of them hurting one of the cowering animals that had the misfortune to live over there.

But the sound came from over to his left in the direction of the electricity substation. Could it be one of the Grid workers, coming in on a Sunday afternoon? He thought it unlikely. Few of them appeared in the week, so a Sunday afternoon visit was most unlikely.

He heard the sound again, a sort of raucous screaming, not unlike that of the jay as it scoured the woods for the bodies of baby birds that have tumbled to their death from their nest. No this sound was more human than animal. The sound repeated, louder, closer this time. It was definitely human, a man's voice.

Who could it be on a Sunday afternoon? Shouting at the top of his voice! Whoever it was, they were ranting like some kind of mad-man!

He felt the hairs on the back of his neck rise slightly. His mouth felt dry and his imagination started to feed him answers. Maybe aliens had landed and they had captured some poor drunk on a park bench and were torturing him!

Whatever or whoever it was they were coming towards him. The shout repeated. Louder still, probably no more than 100 metres from where he sat, destroying the tranquility of his world. What should he do? Normal, friendly people who might somehow have strayed onto the reserve would not present a problem. But none of these would make the noise that this interloper was now producing, screaming abuse at the top of his voice, no more than 50 metres away now, but still screened from view by the trees.

His nerve finally cracked and he decided caution was the better part of valour, scrambling for cover in the nearby long grass at the top of the bank, partially hidden in the small trees and bushes that grew there. Whoever it was, they were following the path, since they made no other obvious sound. If they had been cutting up through the dense woods they would have inevitably crashed about, breaking branches on their way. No this was someone walking steadily along the path, stopping every now and then to shout something at the top of his voice, something that he was very angry about.

He sank lower into the vegetation, fearing what might befall him if spotted by this madman, shouting at the world around him. Then suddenly the man stumbled into view. An old man, well older than his dad, dressed in an old coat, balding, with the thin hairs on the top of his head combed to one side. He obviously had not shaved for several days, his rough short dark beard flecked with grey. He was average in height, a little overweight, with rounded shoulders and a shambling gait as he shuffled along the path below Ben.

Strangely enough he carried two carrier bags and his trousers were soaking wet, as though he had just waded across the river. The most obvious and disturbing thing about him though were his eyes. Dark, hooded depressions in his face, topped by dark bushy eyebrows that met above the bridge of his nose and then continued downward along its ridge.

The man turned in his direction, putting his carrier bags down on the ground next to him. As he did, Ben involuntarily crouched lower in the grass for fear of being spotted. The man's eyes seem to stare at him, but they were obviously looking over Ben's head towards the substation beyond.

Then he slowly raised his fist and shook it at the mass of pylons, wires, insulators, transformers and the like that made up the electricity substation. At the same time he opened his mouth and out came a jumbled mixture of words and oaths, some familiar but forbidden within Ben's family, although fun to repeat with his mates. Others were words he did not know at all, but which he made sure he would remember and try out later. The man was obviously very angry about something.

'Mr. Angry' then went silent again, staring balefully in his direction, his eyes full of malevolent hate. Ben felt himself shudder with fear. This was surely a madman on the loose! What if he was spotted? Would he grab hold of him, ripping his throat out with those horrible nicotine stained teeth that were exposed as he screamed his abuse. Should he run now and hope he could outrun the madman or should he freeze. The latter was easier, but he tensed himself ready to run, just in case he was spotted.

Then, mercifully, the man turned slowly away and continued along the path and out of sight. A minute or so later the screaming repeated, Ben guessed from Dead Elm Drive as it was quieter, more distant this time, but no less frightening. Then the man was gone, his anger apparently abated. Had he gone, or was he hiding somewhere along the path waiting to leap out on Ben?

All caution now cast to the wind Ben stood up, heart pounding and turned towards the substation behind him. Then, in the opposite direction to 'Mr Angry', Ben bolted at full tilt, crashing through the thicket, ignoring the more sensible route along the pathway. He stumbled over the rough ground, brambles clutching at his ankles, branches scratching his face like the clawing fingernails of the madman behind him. He ran as hard as he could, his lungs burning inside his chest.

A pheasant shot out from the long grass next to him, disturbed by his elephantine charge to safety. He almost 'poohed' his pants with fright and then realizing the ridiculousness of what he was doing, he slowed to a more sensible pace and stopped.

He looked around him and listened. No madman was in pursuit. In fact all was tranquility once again. Just the hum of bees and the occasional call of a chaffinch. The world was as it had been, as though nothing had happened. He turned and continued in the opposite direction to that taken by Mr. Angry. His heart was beating more slowly now, his throat sore from his exertions, but his thoughts still racing about his encounter with the screaming madman.

He hoped he never had reason to meet the man again. Little did he realize that Mr. Angry's next intervention would be greatly appreciated.

Chapter Six
The Artist

Ben didn't recognize the man sitting opposite his father, as they talked in his office. However, he could tell from the way they both sat that it was the kind of meeting his father enjoyed, quite different from the all too regular meetings he had with Creamer.

It was a weekday afternoon and Ben had called down to the reserve after school to check out a few things. He wanted to see if the Swans were nesting yet. The visiting school groups had all left by this time and his dad was usually to be found in his office. However, seeing that he was in a meeting, he decided not to disturb him, choosing to walk across to Pylon Bridge to see if he could find the swans' nest. This was usually a large collection of reeds, big enough to hold Sarah as she incubated anything up to 7 enormous eggs for several weeks.

There was no sign of the swans so he returned to the centre, where he found his Dad and his guest leaning against the rails overlooking the lake, still chatting. As Ben arrived, his dad turned to make the introductions.

'Hi Ben. This is Peter. He's a sculptor. Peter, this is my son Ben'

'Hi Ben.' Said Peter 'Pleased to meet you'

Peter had a friendly face and Ben warmed to him immediately.

'Hi' Said Ben politely.

'Our art teacher says a sculptor makes three dimensional art objects. Is that what you do?

'I certainly do' Said Peter

What do you make?' Enquired Ben.

'I like to sculpt using natural materials whenever I can, although I sometimes use metal or plastic to make an impact. I most like creating natural objects, based on things I might find in a place like your nature reserve.'

'What like trees and butterflies?'

'Well a bit like that' Added Peter, 'but I most like to show action, or perhaps conflict, or maybe pose a question to the viewer. Make them think. '

Peter's warm personality, his enthusiasm and excitement whenever he spoke about his work was very engaging. Ben also noticed he had a trace of an accent, but couldn't quite place it. Perhaps he was Scottish? He certainly wasn't from Kent.

'Peter is most interested in the relationship between the nature reserve and the electricity sub-station.' Said

Dad.

Yes, I'm interested in drawing people's attention to the similarities and the differences. I might try and make a tree or an animal out of steel, perhaps constructed like a pylon, with lots of triangular structures'

'People might think you were mad. Trees are not made of triangles'

'No they are not, but it would make them think about it more' Said Peter. 'I can see it's going to be fun working here'

'Working here?' Asked Ben.

'Yes' said Dad 'the Environmental Art Trust are going to pay us for Peter to produce a series of sculptures about the environment and to highlight man's impact upon it.'

'When do you start?' Asked Ben.

'Immediately' Answered Peter. I'm just going to have a walk around the reserve with your father to select the best sites for my work. Do you want to join us?'

'Yes please!' Said Ben.

The three of them returned back to the main nature reserve buildings and then crossed over to Teddy Bear Island to begin the classic tour that his dad always gave to important visitors.

Ben thought how lucky his Dad was to have someone like Peter turn up only a few weeks after Creamer had demanded that he had to raise more money. Things were starting to look up at last.

****

A week later Ben went down to the reserve after school to see how Peter was getting on with his sculpture work. His Dad sent him along The Fox Road, where he said Peter was working. He discovered Peter at the side of the path, surrounded by masses of branches he had lopped off one of the willow trees.

Charlie and the other nature reserve staff had coppiced the oversized and dangerous willow the previous year, by felling its trunk almost down to ground level. Within a year the tree had sprouted brand new, 2-metre long branches from its stump. Peter had removed quite a few of the branches, especially the smaller ones, but he had woven the longest ones into long arm like projections, eight in all. He had also taken some of the branches and fastened their ends together to form a dome like structure in the middle. Ben immediately guessed what he had made.

'It's an octopus!' said Ben admiringly. 'Eight legs and a big rounded body. I love that. And it's all made from a living tree'

'Yes but unfortunately it will not last long. As the branches sprout new side branches, it will soon disappear. That is unless someone who comes here often is prepared to prune back the new growth.' He said, winking at Ben as he did.

'I'll do it' Said Ben 'I come down here all the time'

'That's fine by me, but you'll need to clear it with your dad first as he may not want you using sharp tools. They can be very dangerous. Look at this' Said Peter pulling out a long bladed knife.

'Wow' said Ben 'is it very sharp?'

'What do you think?' Grinned Peter. Whereupon he picked up one of the willow branches lying on the path and proceeded to remove the side branches with the minimum of effort.

'A blunt knife could have done the same job, but I would be pretty tired after a day's work. A sharp knife is essential for my work. A sharp knife is also safer to use, as long as it's used with care, because it is so easy to use. A blunt knife needs more pressure so may accidentally slip. And then who knows what?' He added.

Ben was impressed with the knife. But he had more questions to ask this fascinating character. 'Are you going to make something else?' Asked Ben. 'You said you liked to mix natural and man-made things'

'Well I have already been planning one.' Said Peter. 'I just needed your Dad's agreement. Happily he has approved my plans. In fact it was you that gave me the idea when we first met, a giant bird made like a steel pylon. I've also decided where to put it.'

'Where?' Asked Ben.

'Just follow me.' He said and led Ben down to Knackers' Hole.

'This is the place, right next to the main road, between it and the substation. Would you consider lending me a hand?'

'Yes please. But isn't this a rather noisy place to put it?'

'I agree, but I reckon thousands of cars pass this point every day, so lots of people will get to see it. Do you want to know what it will look like? Because it just so happens that I have got a sketch of the work here' And Peter pulled a piece of folded paper out of his pocket.

On the paper he had sketched the vague likeness of a bird, posed a bit like a blackbird foraging for food on the ground. Its head was up and to one side, as though it were listening for a strange sound, but its pointed beak was angled downwards ready to strike the next creature that should happen to get in its path.

'Pretty fierce beast' whistled Ben 'I wouldn't like to get in the way of that beak!'

'No' Said Peter 'But don't worry he'll be well fastened down'

Instead of feathers and a solid body, Peter had drawn the bird as a series of triangular shaped 'boxes' made up of angle iron or lengths of wood.

'It looks like a cross between a pylon and a bird'

Enthused Ben.

'That's right.' Said Peter 'In fact I think that would be a good name for it 'The Pylon Bird', but tell me one thing Ben, why is this area called Knackers' Hole? It's a rather odd name'

'Oh that's because across the road there,' said Ben pointing across the main road that ran alongside the reserve here, 'there used to be an abattoir or knackers' yard, where farm animals were taken to be slaughtered and then sent to butcher's shops to be carved up into meat.'

'I see' Said Peter 'A bit grizzly then. Personally I don't agree with eating meat. I'm a vegan. In fact I hate the whole idea of killing or hurting animals. I think it's worse than killing people.' As he said this Ben couldn't help but notice a flash of anger in his eyes. Just a fleeting one, but he quite clearly felt very strongly about the subject.

Ben said, 'I don't like people who hurt animals either, including the kids across the river who play at shooting at birds with air pistols, but I don't agree with those people who break into places and set animals free either'

'Oh really? Why not? Tell me' Quizzed Peter.

'Some people break into mink farms and let all the mink escape. It's partly because of escaped mink that the reserve hasn't got any water voles and that Sebastian and Sarah's cygnets don't often survive more than a few weeks.'

'I can see you know a great deal about the subject, young fella. I reckon you are going to be a great help to me. I need a wildlife expert for advice.' Smiled Peter.

'Great' Said Ben 'But I'd best be going now, otherwise Mum will be wondering where I've got to. I said I'd be home for tea.'

'I've finished here.' Said Peter 'So I'll walk you back to the car park'

Peter and Ben chatted amiably as they returned to the car park, where his Dad was waiting to drive him home. As Ben got into his father's car he looked to see what car Peter drove. He was both surprised and impressed when he saw Peter don black motorcycle leathers and helmet, kick-start a large motorbike and drive off, with a wave of his hand. Ben liked Peter.

Chapter Seven
The Roundhouse

Today was a special day. Ben, his dad and all the nature reserve staff, including their supervisor Charlie, were gathered in CanterburyWoods to start on a big building project.

Charlie was a large man, in his sixties. He had been working at Broad Oak Lakes for over 20 years and there was little he didn't know about the place. In the wintertime he generally grew a beard, which was near white in colour. The other staff often laughingly suggested he dress up as Santa Claus as a winter money-making attraction. He always took these jibes in good spirit, being a man of mild manners.

From Easter onwards the beard was removed and he resorted to the wearing of shorts, the biggest and baggiest that you have ever seen. Come rain or shine this was his attire until the end of October, when jeans and whiskers took over.

One of Dad's money-making schemes was to generate income from the many tourists who visited Canterbury each summer. He had a vision to commercialize the nature reserve to attract more people. Ben had been horrified at the idea, until his dad explained that they were not turning the place into a theme park for tourists, but to open the reserve as a place of calm for any members of the public prepared to pay for it. Part of his plan was to add features to enhance the natural environment of the reserve, such as bird hides, bridges, walkways and sculptures.

One of the proposed features was the building of a 'Celtic' roundhouse, out of local timber. When Ben saw the plans he was excited about the idea, especially as a den for him to play in. Ben had always liked building dens, but none of his had ever lasted more than a few weeks. However, the roundhouse was to be a permanent feature of the reserve. So here they all were during the quiet of the May holiday period, preparing to build.

A ring of post-holes had already been dug in a clearing in the woods. A pile of some twenty or so chestnut stakes were stacked to one side, each being about one and a half metres long, ready to drop into the holes. Along side these was a further stack of longer poles for the roof trusses. These would all sit on the shorter poles, meeting in the middle of the roof they were to support.

Smaller, thinner poles would lock these big trusses together. Finally the whole structure would be covered with thatch, using bundles of reeds cut from the nature reserve's own reed beds. These were stacked well away from the building site, forming an enormous mound of bundles of giant straw-like grass.

During the morning Ben was kept busy holding the shorter posts whilst Charlie and the other men packed the earth around their bases to hold them firm. By lunchtime most of the posts were in place. The men all threw their tools into a wheelbarrow and set off back to the main buildings for their ritual 'cuppa'. Ben however had decided to stay and have his sandwiches in the woods.

After a short lunch in Kingfisher Hide, watching the coots and moorhens going about their daily chores, he decided to walk up towards the far end of the reserve to East Pond and see if he could spot any of the Great Crested Newts that he knew liked to live there.

Ben still had reservations about this area of the reserve, since his encounter with Mr. Angry. However, as he gazed into the waters of the pond, the voice he heard walking up the trail from the direction of the lakes, was a familiar one. His Dad had told him that he would be leading a group of adults on a tour of the reserve. The sound of his father's voice grew closer as they ambled in the sunshine towards the benches at Butterfly Bank.

'Right' said Dad, 'time for a break in the tour. Hopefully you all have your packed lunches with you. This is an excellent place to take lunch. Just take a seat on any of the benches and enjoy the sun for the next 20 minutes or so. Is that alright with you Erica?' He addressed a woman at the head of the group, whom Ben assumed to be the group's leader.

'Yes Mr. Franklin, this will do nicely.' She responded sweetly.

She was a fairly short, dumpy looking woman probably in her forties, her brown hair arranged in a short bob around her rounded features. She was dressed rather elegantly, in a dark two-piece suit. Rather inappropriately for a field trip Ben thought, although she had made the concession of wearing an expensive looking pair of riding boots.

'Hello Ben.' Said his Dad as Ben climbed up from the pond. 'Lurking in the bushes again?'

'Hi Dad' Said Ben.

'This is my son, Ben.' He announced to the woman leading the group.

'Hello my dear' She replied.

'What are you all here for?' Enquired Ben, always interested to know what brought people to look at the reserve.

'Oh we're here courtesy of my father I suppose.' She replied. 'He's president of 'The League Against Animals for Cosmetic and Medical Testing'. He wasn't able to come himself, but he wanted the league's members to benefit from the wonderful work being carried out here by your father. I must say it is nice to see animals where they belong – in the wild and not in a laboratory.'

Ben couldn't help noticing how intense her expression became as she delivered her speech, as though she was on a soapbox surrounded by thousands of admirers.

'Dad can I show you the Great Crested Newts in the pond?' asked Ben.

'Sure' Said his Dad. 'Please excuse us Erica.' And they made their way down to the water's edge.

As Ben pointed out the newts he asked his dad about the group. 'They're a funny bunch, why are they so interested in the reserve?'

'Yes I agree. An unlikely looking bunch of wildlife enthusiasts' His Dad commented, 'Especially the leader. She's Erica Butler. Her father's the well-known Canterbury millionaire. Made all his money from property deals in East Kent. The strangest thing about her is that she keeps asking questions about the substation, how secure it is, what the different bits do, is it occupied all the time. You would think she was casing the joint with the intention of stealing the electricity from it one day!' He laughed.

After 10 minutes of newt watching and eating their sandwiches, Dad decided it was time to get back to his group. As they climbed up to join the group gathered on the benches, Ben noticed that Erica Butler was at the top of the hill, with her back to the group. She was looking intently over the hill towards the substation. This was where Ben had been hiding when he first met Mr. Angry. As she turned around he noticed that she had a camera in her hands. She had evidently been photographing the substation compound.

Ben thought nothing more of the incident and said goodbye to his father, before making his way back towards the roundhouse, to help the conservation team get to work on the rest of the roundhouse.

As he walked he played over in his mind the number of strange characters who appeared to be visiting the reserve lately. First there was Mr. Angry, then the policeman and his dog, then Creamer, now this woman taking photos of the substation, even Peter. But he liked Peter and saw him as a friend. Still all this outside interest in the substation was a little unnerving. How many more strange characters were likely to be drawn to this magical place?

****

Next day the whole team was out again building the roundhouse. The activity was obviously good for the team's morale in the face of all the pressures from City Hall.

The posts were now well bedded in, with the rammed earth holding them tight. As the day progressed, the team fitted the roof trusses, radiating out from a central pole, to give the building its general roundhouse shape for the first time.

By the time 5 o'clock arrived, Charlie and his team put all the tools into a wheelbarrow and trundled them back to the nature reserve buildings, leaving Ben to admire the day's labours. He was well pleased with what they had achieved and couldn't wait for it to be finished so that he could spend a night in it. Of course he would have to work hard on Mum and Dad to let him stay even one night in it.

Over the next few days the team fitted cross supports, added woven hazel wattle walls and covered the roof with reed thatch.

On the last day barrow-loads of sticky mud were trundled over from the lake and mixed with chopped reed stems and cement powder. This was then daubed onto the hazel wattle, with the expectation of it setting solid to give the mud walls of the finished roundhouse.

As the day drew to an end, the team performed the final ceremony, cutting the central support pillar. Chainsaw in hand, Charlie climbed the step-ladder supported by one of the other men and sliced through the 10 centimetre upright, leaving the weight of the roof supported by the walls alone. A great cheer went up and everyone shook hands with everyone else.

The nature reserve now had a large circular space into which 30 children could be crammed for story telling or just to shelter from the rain. But to Ben it was a den, a place of retreat. It was his place.

****

'So, to what do I owe the pleasure of this meeting?' asked Smith.

He and Cyclops were sitting in Canterbury's rather ancient cinema, watching the latest Matrix film. It was Cyclops' choice of rendezvous. Smith never ceased to be amused by his obvious sense of humour.

'I hope you don't expect me to walk up walls when I work for you.' Laughed Smith.

'It might help' whispered Cyclops. He was sitting directly behind Smith, having entered the cinema half way through the film. Smith tried to ignore the film's action, but had been rather enjoying the plot until his boss's arrival. The morning matinee showing of the film, its last day at Canterbury, guaranteed that they would have the cinema largely to themselves. They sat in the least popular seats at the back left hand side of the auditorium. Two teenagers and a father with his young son were the only others present, far away towards the front.

At least the darkened auditorium and the ear splitting soundtrack of the film would conceal their discussions, even two grown men sitting close together in the dark might raise eyebrows in some quarters.

'How's your progress with the substation?' Enquired Cyclops

'Things are coming along nicely, now that you've called off your man with his dog. My own cover is pretty well sorted now. I've also managed to make contact with our friend Miss Butler at long last.' He replied.

'You have? Well that's a step in the right direction'

'Nothing conclusive yet, but she wants me to get involved in a 'project', as she calls it.

'OK. You know what you're doing but you need to be

particularly careful in the light of some information we've just picked up. Two or three months ago Immigration informed us that Michael Kelly had been spotted entering the country.' Said Cyclops. 'He's gone to ground since, but he makes me feel a little uneasy.'

'Kelly?' Whispered Smith. He was aware of the man's reputation as the man credited with planting some of the IRA's deadliest bombs during their campaign of terror 20 or 30 years earlier.

'I thought he was locked up?'

'No, he was released several months ago. Part of the government's attempts to normalise the situation in Northern Ireland. It may be nothing, but he's never renounced violence and our intelligence is that he is linked to a former IRA splinter group.'

'But what does he have to do with me?' Asked Smith.

'I don't know exactly, but recent information we've received suggests that the group in question have been offering to sell their services to anyone interested in their particular skills, particularly bomb-making. One or two groups have been linked with them, including suspected Animal Liberation Front activists. Kelly is just the sort of person that your animal rights terrorist friends might hire. If, as we suspect, they are looking to carry out a raid in the near future, his bomb-making expertise could be what they are looking for.' Said Cyclops.

'What do you want me to do' Asked Smith.

'Carry on as you are, but just be careful, you could be dealing with something bigger than we initially expected. Mind how you go'

At this Cyclops got up and melted into the darkness at the back of the cinema. Smith returned to the film action, wondering about the significance of Kelly and how he was to find out if he was in some way involved with future developments at Broad Oak Lakes.

As he watched the film, Smith mused over the fact that the Agent Smith in the Matrix seemed to have much better luck than him, when it came to gathering information about his enemies.

Chapter Eight
The Fisher Thief

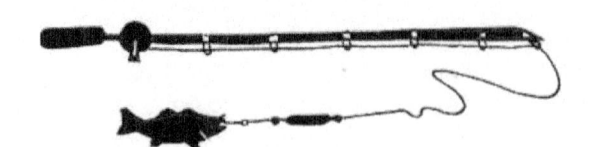

As May turned to June, Ben occasionally decided to get up very early and join Lizzie for a dawn trek around the lakes. The sun was just starting to light up the nature reserve and the birds were in full voice.

Amongst the early morning bird sounds ringing across the lakes were the grumbling calls of reed warblers and the melodic fluting of a blackbird. The most distinctive bird song of all was that of the Cetti's Warbler. This small bird sat in a tall willow or alder tree being perfectly silent for several minutes. Then it would release a torrent of noise '"What's my name? Cettis! Cettis! Cettis! That's it!"

No matter how often he heard it, Ben always jumped with surprise. Today was no exception, causing Lizzie to burst out laughing.

'Noisy or what?' Lizzie laughed. 'Lets go and see if Sebastian and Sarah have had their cygnets yet.'

'We'll not be able to approach the nest from Ant Island, otherwise the swan's might set on us. Let's go over Long Bridge and try to get a view from the Sluice Gate' said Ben.

As they crossed Long Bridge they could see that their luck was in, as four small grey fluffy balls were being fussed over by Sarah in the gigantic nest both swans had built in the reeds only a few weeks earlier. They were about to move round to the Sluice Gate for a better view when Ben saw a movement off to their right.

'What's that' whispered Ben. 'I thought I saw something move over there.'

'Where?' said Lizzie.

'By the Sluice Gate' He said pointing to where he had seen the movement.

'I can't see anything'

'I'm sure someone is down there, probably one of those fishermen that sneak over the fence. Lets get a bit closer and see if we can spy on them' Ben set off half crouching, probably convinced that he would make an excellent Indian tracker, stopping every few seconds to wave Lizzie on and holding up his finger to his lips to indicate that she had to move quietly.

As they stalked towards the Sluice Gate a moorhen shot out of the sedge growing at the lake margin. As the bird ran across the surface of the water, its wings flapping and its whole demeanor seeming to be that of Chicken Licken screaming 'the sky's fallen in, the sky's fallen in!' Ben cursed their clumsy movements.

'If someone is down there, they'll know we're coming

now' said Lizzie, a big grin across her face.

Ben shot her a cross look, feeling the blood rush of embarrassment filling his face. As they got within view of the Sluice Gate it was obvious that whoever had been there had now gone. The ground adjacent to the outflow was well trampled. It looked pretty recent, although it could have been the result of one of the reserve staff checking for blockages in the pipe that allowed water to flow out of the lake and into the river here.

As they inched down to the water's edge Ben and Lizzie looked into the water. There, reflected in the clear water of the lake, Ben saw 2 pale blue eyes looking into his. With a start he turned round, grabbing Lizzie's arm as he did.

'Looking for something?' Came the rasping voice of the eyes' owner, a man probably in his 70's. Ben and Lizzie stood up, more than a little alarmed by the way this wizened old man had crept up on them without a sound. 'Perhaps I can help?'

'It's private property here you know' said Ben rather obviously.

'I know. I reckon it's a fair cop though Hiawatha. You tracked me down and what chance does an old man like me have against two such masters of jungle warfare?' A smile lit up his eyes, which became even more creased by the action. Then he laughed such a hearty laugh that even the alarmed Ben and Lizzie couldn't help but smile at him.

'Who are you?' said Lizzie as forthright as ever, having

recovered her composure more quickly than Ben.

'Me? Oh I'm just a poacher. Well I'm trying to be, but unless I catch something I suppose I'm really a failed poacher, especially as I've just been caught by the bailiffs' He chuckled. 'You're not really going to turn me in are you? I don't think I'd survive a spell in prison'

Despite his apparent guilt, Ben and Lizzie both warmed to this little old man who seemed to have scant respect for the laws of trespass. 'Been here all night I have and not got a bite, so I'm afraid there's nothing for you to confiscate. Who are you anyway? Haven't seen you round here before young fella.'

'My dad is the new manager'

At this the old man whistled through his rather yellowed and twisted teeth. 'Gone and got yourself into some real trouble now you have Danny boy' he muttered to himself. 'What you going to do now?'

'Nothing' said Ben, a bit unsure of himself.

'Tell you what. I'll make a deal with you. If you let me off this time, I'll share half of what I've got with you.' He said as he patted his hands over his jacket to see what he might offer by way of a bribe. 'Sorry no fish, but you can have half of this Mars Bar if you like.'

Ben and Lizzie were a bit unsure; their parent's having told them not to take sweets from strangers. However, there was something in old Dan's eyes and the kindly way in which he spoke that convinced them he was harmless.

Old Dan tore the bar in two and handed half to Ben and the remainder to Lizzie. As he sat down on the concrete capping to the sluice gate, the two youngsters relaxed and sat down on the grass.

'Been fishing these lakes for 60 years now, ever since they were first carved out of the ground. I can tell you a few stories about this place. Would you like to hear any?'

'Yes please.' They both said eagerly.

'OK then. Just make yourselves comfortable and I'll begin' Said Danny.

Danny was one of those people able to spin a yarn. At times fact and fiction seemed to melt into each other. He told them all about the old days when the lake was first dug, his own childhood experiences on the site, the use of the lakes as a dump after the destruction of large parts of the city during its Second World War bombing, the building of the substation in the 1960s and the eventual creation of the nature reserve in the 1970s. He'd seen it all.

Danny also told them about some of the characters they were likely to meet on the reserve. These included illegal fishermen like himself, who were largely harmless and rarely caught anything in the lake. He told them about the gypsy folk who sometimes used the reserve as cover when stealing things from warehouses that backed onto the reserve.

'Crafty bunch they are. Some are a bit ugly though, like old Scarface. Been known to break into places like the builders yard over there.' Said Danny, indicating in the direction of Canterbury Woods. 'Not daft that lot. They hide the stolen stuff in the lake for a few weeks afterwards and only come back to collect it once things have died down a bit, rather than risk being caught with it whilst it's still hot.'

Ben told Danny he had already met the character he called 'Mr Angry'.

'Oh he's a pretty harmless character' Danny explained ' He lives in an old caravan next to the industrial estate on the other side of the reserve.'

Apparently he had once been in an argument with the substation's owners, 'The Grid', at some stage in the past, which explained his attitude towards the substation and why he would stop and rant in that direction as he walked through the reserve.

'So you've met him already? Well the only danger you might face from him is if he were to offer you a sweet'

'Why? What would he do to me?' Said Ben with real concern.

'Oh he won't do anything to you' Winked Old Ben 'It's just that any sweet he has in his pocket has probably been there for years, mixed up with snotty handkerchiefs, bits of old chewing gum, slugs and other horrible things. You are most likely to die of food poisoning' He laughed. 'Not like these' He said pulling out another chocolate bar for each of them.

They both accepted the gifts gleefully; although Ben

double-checked the sell-by date on his when Danny wasn't looking.

But it was his story about the Monster of the Lake that they liked best. By the time he had finished the story and answered all their questions about this mythical fish that Danny had been trying to catch for 50 years, it was approaching lunch-time.

'I'm afraid I have to go now.' Announced Lizzie.

'Me too.' Said Ben.

'Yes off you go young 'uns. Its time I was getting home also. See you another day. But just you watch out for the monster, there's no saying when he might appear and he might just fancy a piece of tender young un like one of you two.' He cackled with delight.

As they walked away, Ben said to Lizzie 'You don't really believe that story about the monster do you'

'Of course not, but it's a good story isn't it?' Agreed Lizzie, with an appreciative smile.

As they reached the Long Bridge they both turned to wave to Danny.

'He's gone.' Said Lizzie with surprise. 'Appeared out of thin air and now disappeared back into it. How does he move so quickly?'

'Beats me' Said Ben 'perhaps he's as unreal as the monster?'

Laughing they made there way over the bridge, whilst in the dark water below a large pair of malevolent eyes watched them with considerable interest.

Chapter Nine
Cross-country Capers

It was early July. With the growing pressure from City Hall and Creamer in particular, Dad had to find extra income from somewhere to ensure the future of the nature reserve. The recent foot-and-mouth scare had prevented the local schools' cross-country competition from taking place at its usual venue.

Broad Oak Lakes was offered as an alternative venue, with sponsorship, advertising and sales income promised as a result of the event's high profile locally. Several hundred children from five local secondary schools crammed into the reserve to take part in the event or to spectate. Ben's school, St Augustine's, was one of the schools taking part. Ben had earned himself a place in the under 14 boys' race. He was the youngest runner from his school, the only member of Year 8 to make the team, with the rest being drawn from Year 9.

Mr Grant, the school's PE teacher took him and the rest of the team to one side and spoke to them encouragingly. 'We have a real chance of winning this one, but you all have to perform as a team. I know Ben is only Year 8 and it's unlikely that he will win the race, or even make the top 10, but he has a vital role to play as well. Let me remind you of the scoring system. Each team member scores points equal to his position in the race.'

'What does that mean?' Asked one of the lads.

Well. If John comes first', he said indicating towards the best runner in the team, 'Then he would be awarded one point.' He used his index finger to accentuate the point. 'Likewise, if Ben were to come in 20th, then he would score 20 points. At the end of the race each team's points will be totaled up, with the winning team being the one with the least number of points.'

'So Ben might cost us the race?' Groaned one of the others.

'No. As easily the youngest runner in the team, I'm realistically expecting him to be the lowest placed member of the team. If Ben does come at least 20th out of the 25 runners, then we will be well placed to take the trophy.' Mr. Grant explained. 'However, I'm expecting all of you to beat Ben. If you don't, then it will be one of you that will have cost us the race, not Ben!'

As the crowd of twenty-five 12 and 13 year olds lined up at the start of the race, Ben could feel the nerves gripping him, as the butterflies in his stomach fluttered around. He felt almost sick with anticipation as he looked around at everyone else.

'Right lads just do your best, and remember that every place counts.' Said Mr. Grant encouragingly.

Finally he whispered to Ben. 'Don't worry about your position too much Ben. Most of all make sure you finish the race, otherwise the whole team is disqualified'.

As they lined up, the rest of his team, in fact every boy competing, looked as ashen faced as Ben. It was a fine dry day, with a largely overcast sky and temperatures that the spectators might describe as pleasant. However, every one of the twenty-five shaking young men thought it was cold and wished he was just a spectator.

As Ben looked around him he saw one face he recognized. It was one of the air-gun kids from across the river. He was dressed in the blue colours of St Vincent's High. Ben had seen and heard them several times in the past. On one occasion, whilst they were shooting at coots in the River Stour, he had shouted for them to stop, but they had just laughed at him, saying 'We'll shoot you next time'.

Afterwards Ben had reflected on what the police officer at Felixstowe had said about notifying the police, rather than getting directly involved. Why did Ben attract trouble he wondered?

The air-gun kid was slightly taller than Ben, with close-cropped hair and an unpleasant threatening look about him. As Ben looked at him he noticed that he was talking to two other boys. Neither of them was dressed in running kit, being there just to spectate, like the kids from his own school. He vaguely recognized them too, realizing that they were the other two kids who had been shooting at birds. One of the boys, a small, but nonetheless threatening looking individual, pointed at Ben. His friend, the one who was taking part in the race, immediately turned and looked straight at Ben. A mischievous smile ran across his face. Ben immediately looked the other way and turned his attention to Mr. Grant's final words of encouragement.

'Right, you're about to start. Remember you are a team and give it your best. We have a very good chance of winning this if you perform to your best.' Said Mr. Grant.

As they lined up at the start line, which had been drawn on the grass of the Gridlands field, Ben found himself next to the blue shirted bird shooter.

'Don't expect your nice green shirt to be clean by the end of the race pretty boy. You'll be eating mud soon' He said menacingly.

'Stuff him, Josh' shouted one of his friends from the crowd.

Ben just looked at Josh and realized he'd probably made an enemy. He didn't have time to respond, even if he could have found the words, as the starter called them to their marks.

'On your marks …'

'Plenty of those on you soon.' Came the menacing whisper.

'Get set ….'

'To eat dirt' Josh added.

'Bang!' Went the starter's gun.

Immediately 25 pairs of legs took their first stride on the two-mile course around the reserve. However, Ben's second stride failed to follow-on from his first. His blue shirted neighbour deliberately nudged him off-balance, causing his right foot to become hooked around his left knee. As the twenty-four other boys belted off towards the main substation access road, Ben found himself face down on the grass, counting daisies.

'Come on Ben' Shouted Mr. Grant. 'You can do it'

As Ben pulled himself up off the short mown turf and set off in pursuit of the others, Josh turned and grinned at Ben. 'Plenty more where that came from'.

The field was already becoming stretched out as some of the faster boys tore off down the road towards Pylon Picnic Site. As Ben closed on the back-markers of the pack ahead, they had to turn off the road and hurdle a low fence. He had already made up ground on his blue shirted rival, who already seemed uncomfortable with the pace set by the others. As they jumped the hurdle Ben felt a ripple of pleasure, from having already caught up with his antagonist.

However, his enthusiasm was his undoing. As they turned sharp right into Pylon Path, Ben realized it was a trap. One of Josh's lackeys was waiting by the hedge. With Josh on his left he had no chance of escaping the extended leg in front of him. Down he went again. This time the ground was not so soft and forgiving. As he stuck his arms out in front of him, to break his fall, his outstretched palms took the brunt of his momentum. He managed to roll over, but as he pulled himself to his feet he felt a stinging pain in the heels of his hands and his knees. He paused to inspect the damage and realized he was bleeding where his skin had made contact with the gravel path.

Limping with the pain, Ben felt close to tears, not so much from the pain but the indignation of being a victim. Twice!

Once again he saw the grinning blue shirted figure disappearing down the course.

'Why don't you give up?' Taunted the boy who had tripped him.

But this remark had quite the opposite effect on the resolute Ben. Determined to at least finish the race, he set off once more in hot pursuit, his shirt already a mix of mud, blood and grass stains from his falls.

Ben decided to take the first lap around the lakes more gently, confident that some of the faster starters would tire. By the time he reached Dead Dog's Bridge he had already passed four other walking runners complaining of 'stitch'. As he reached Electric Avenue, with its views over the substation, the blue shirted shape of Josh was only a few metres ahead of him. Here was his chance to pass him, before the course narrowed towards Great Crested Newt Pond.

He was about to surge passed him, when something caught his eye, causing him to slow. Down by the substation, adjacent to the off-limits electric fencing was a smartly dressed man, complete with shiny leather shoes and a long black coat. He was looking intently at part of the substation. He was obviously not a member of the Grid staff, since he was neither dressed in the regulation hard-hat, nor was he wearing Grid marked clothing. Perhaps he was just one of the visiting school teachers, who had somehow got lost on the reserve. Whoever he was he was inappropriately dressed, his mud caked shoes indicating that he had no idea what sensible people wear for a walk around a nature reserve.

Thinking no more about it, Ben returned to the task in hand, to overtake his newly acquired rival ahead of him. With a turn of pace that surprised Ben, he shot past the struggling Josh, treating himself to a grin as he looked over his shoulder. The other boy just glared.

By now Ben reckoned he must be about 19th or 20th in the race as he picked his way along the muddy path below Substation Surprise and then across the car park, where the second lap of the course began. About 30 metres ahead of him he could see two other boys. By the time he reached Invader's Grove he felt confident of catching them, as they followed the downhill stretch towards Alder Tree Jetty.

One of the boys was dressed in the red running vest of Barnes Court, the other was in the blue of St Vincent's High. Few spectators had bothered to walk to this part of the course. However, to Ben's surprise two familiar figures were standing on the jetty. As the boy in red pulled alongside the St. Vincent's boy, the smaller of the two spectators suddenly stepped into his path.

'Sorry.' Said the smaller boy, grinning from ear to ear.

'You little sod.' Shouted the obstructed boy.

At this his much bigger friend took a step towards him. 'I think you should say sorry' He said, making a threatening gesture with his fist.

The boy in red, looked around him, realized he was at a big disadvantage without a friend in sight and muttered 'Sorry'.

The bigger boy continued to obstruct his path until the smaller one added 'Let him go. Look who's coming now.' Pointing in the direction of Ben.

The boy in red made his escape, with considerable relief, as the two proceeded to stand across Ben's path. He paused momentarily. Behind him he could here another runner approaching. Hoping that in the face of another runner they would back down, he turned to wait, only to see the blue shirt of Josh appear at the top of the slope. He was now trapped between the two waiting for him at Alder Tree Jetty and the onrushing Josh.

'Lets put him in the lake.' Shouted the smaller boy.

Ben's heart sank as he realized his predicament. However, instead of his fear causing him to freeze in his boots, it had the opposite effect. As the adrenalin kicked in, Ben's brain reacted. Fighting was not an option, as he was heavily outnumbered. He could see no way past the two blocking his path ahead of him, whilst the onrushing Josh had the advantage of the slope.

Fortunately Ben had the benefit of local knowledge. Only a few day's earlier he had been helping Charlie and the rest of the conservation team to create a new path that bypassed Alder Tree Jetty. Quick as a flash he shot up through the recently cleared bramble thicket. The onrushing Josh tried to adjust himself and follow Ben. The other two realizing he was about to escape, also raced up the hill after him. Off balance, the speeding Josh could do nothing but continue downhill and collide with his two friends, the three of them ending up in a heap on the ground.

With a burst of energy he had no idea he still possessed, Ben shot along the newly cleared path until it rejoined the main route at Heron Path. Behind him he could hear raised voices.

'You stupid gits. Get out of my way.' Came Josh's voice.

By the time they had untangled themselves, Ben had been able to put a good 50 metres between them. He also knew the course well enough to realize that none of them would have the opportunity of blocking him again.

His energy renewed by the adrenalin rush of the earlier confrontation, Ben careered through Canterbury Woods and along Jungle Walk. As he approached Long Bridge, a crowd of spectators stood watching.

'Come on Ben' shouted a familiar voice, as his Dad encouraged him on.

Ben was really flying now as he overtook the red and the blue vested runners he had seen earlier at Alder Tree Jetty.

'You're in seventeenth place Ben.' Encouraged Mr. Grant. 'Keep that up and we should win the team race'.

Full of running he picked his way along the path, past the Sluice Gate, along Campion Path and over Dead Dog's Bridge. The track was its usual mire as it climbed up past Dead Elm Drive to Butterfly Bank. This was the heaviest part of the course, with the slope and the clinging mud conspiring to drag down weary limbs. The adrenalin of his earlier confrontation was now wearing off, as was the encouragement he had received from the spectators.

Nonetheless he was able to pass one runner who had fallen foul of the mud, whilst Ben had taken the less muddy option up the hill. Home advantage was certainly paying off for him today. Passing further runners just pushed him on still faster.

As he reached the highest part of the course at Electric Avenue, for the second time, he reckoned he was probably in fifteenth place and felt certain he could ensure his team won. Then he caught sight of the smartly dressed trespasser he had spotted earlier down by the electric fencing. What was he doing? Who was he?

As he passed the bird hide at Energy Heights he had an idea. He knew that an old pair of binoculars was kept chained to the wall, for the use of visitors. He stopped, pulled back the bolt on the door and dashed into the hide. Grabbing hold of the binoculars he focused them on the immaculately dressed figure below him.

Immediately the back of the man's head shot into close-up. As the man turned into profile he could see that he was taking photographs of the substation equipment, especially the transformers that hummed in the far corner. As he watched, the man turned towards Ben and put his camera down, giving him a clear view of a thin faced man, with neatly styled hair and dark rimmed, tinted glasses.

Committing the man's face to memory, Ben's thoughts returned to the race and the fact that his team was depending on him to finish. He dropped the binoculars, letting them dangle on their chain, as he heard several sets of feet plod past him.

He threw open the bird hide door and ran slap into the surprised form of Josh. Josh was thrown into the tall patch of stinging nettles growing across the path from the bird hide.

'You little sod!' he shouted, followed by other less acceptable expressions, as he staggered into the mass of tall stems and leaves covered in tiny stinging hairs.

'Sorry.' Grinned Ben' as he turned and continued running down the track towards Rock Down.

Buoyed up by getting his revenge on his enemy he was able to pass the two runners who had overtaken him whilst he was in the bird hide. As he entered the car park for the second and last time he saw Lizzie waving at him. As he drew close to her he could see her pointing behind him and shouting. 'Run Ben'.

As he looked round he could see the figure of Josh only a few strides behind him. His face was a picture of determination and anger, his legs already showing the raised red bumps caused by his excursion into the nettle patch. Josh was obviously determined to overtake Ben.

Ben was equally determined to beat Josh. As they both raced along the final road section of the course towards the finish at Gridlands, Josh pulled alongside Ben. As they ran they both glared at each other, hardly noticing the other runners they passed, as they gave every ounce of energy in their quest to beat each other.

With only about 20 metres to go, Josh started flagging and Ben could feel himself pulling slightly ahead of his adversary. He hardly had chance to savour the prospect of victory when a rabbit shot out from the undergrowth and stood frozen to the spot, terrified, in front of the two on-rushing boys.

Seeing the startled look on the creatures face, Ben broke his stride momentarily and stepped around it. The maneuver took only a split second to effect, but with Josh showing no interest in the rabbit's fate, he kept his momentum, pulling slightly ahead of Ben.

Ben dug deep, determined to win, but with the finish line only a few strides away, the result was inevitable, with Josh dipping over the line a fraction of a second ahead of him.

The crowd erupted with excitement at the sprint finish. Josh and Ben both collapsed with exhaustion. Ben's throat was burning, he was gulping air as though it was going out of fashion and he could feel a searing pain in the side of his chest. Worst of all was the realization that he had lost.

Mr. Grant rushed up to him and dragged him to his feet. 'Well done Ben' he shouted. 'I didn't know you had it in you. Where did that sprint finish come from?'

'Don't know' gasped Ben. 'I'm sorry I let him beat me'

As he straightened up he found himself looking straight into the triumphant eyes of Josh. The other boy looked hard at him, pointed his right hand index finger at him and mouthed the words 'Got you'.

'Yes he may have beaten you' said Mr. Grant, 'but that final sprint took you into 10th place. Thanks to you, and your friend over there for driving you so hard, we got all our team into the top ten. Now we are certain of winning the team competition.'

As this news sank in, the rest of his team gathered round him and slapped him on the back, whooping and cheering. They then picked him up and paraded around with him on their shoulders.

Once again he caught sight of his main adversary of the day, surrounded by his two henchmen. As they looked in his direction, Josh made his fingers into the shape of a gun and pointed at him menacingly. Ben was obviously going to have to be careful not to run into them again.

As his team paraded up and down, cheered on by spectators from his school, Ben caught sight of the stranger dressed in the long black coat and the shiny black leather shoes. He was standing by a black Mercedes, cleaning spatters of mud off with a cloth. He was obviously not a happy man on a nature reserve, where dirt was the norm. So what was he doing here, taking photographs of the substation?

It had been quite a day for Ben, with lots of incident and final success. But it was the behaviour of the mysterious stranger that was uppermost in his mind as he went to bed that evening. Here was yet another strange visitor to the reserve showing unusual interest in the substation. What was going on?

Chapter Ten
The Monster of Broad Oak Lake

As the early morning sun threw its piercing blue rays into the sky, a thin mist hovered over the lake. Ben and Lizzie were sitting at Cygnet Point, rods in hand, watching the wildlife. The coots were up early patrolling their territory as usual.

'How reassuring it must be to have to work such regular hours' Said Ben, 'Sunrise, sunset, day in day out'

'Yes 'cooting' must have its rewards' Added Lizzie.

'Kingfisher!' shouted Ben as a flash of blue caught his eye, nothing more, but he instinctively knew it must have been a kingfisher flashing low over the water.

'Well done' said Lizzie with real admiration in her voice. Six months earlier he wouldn't have even noticed it, let alone know what it was. How much he had learned about the place and how much he obviously loved it.

'Wow' said Lizzie, the words punctuating the early morning air and causing more than one startled frog to plop back into the lake. 'I never tire of seeing Kingfishers'

Here at Cygnet Point they knew they would have the benefit of the first rays of sun on the reserve, sitting quietly, rods in hand, to see what they might catch.

Charlie, the reserve's handyman, had told Ben that it was a good location for pike fishing, with the occasional 20-pounder being landed.

As with Old Dan, in-fact all fishermen, Charlie was not averse to telling anyone who would listen, stories of the monster pike that had supposedly eluded capture for nearly 30 years. Ben did not disappoint, as he listened to every word as though it were gospel. Fuelled with stories from both Charlie and Old Dan, Ben and Lizzie were out next morning rods in hand hoping to land the beast.

As the sun finally threw its warming light onto their faces, Lizzie declared, 'We've been sitting watching these floats for over an hour'. Not being natural fishermen they were growing restless from the inactivity.

'Shall we pack our things and head back home?' said Ben.

But before Lizzie had time to answer, Ben's float dipped beneath the water.

For a fraction of a second they both just stared at where the float had been, then just in time Ben grabbed his rod, as the line started zipping off into the water in pursuit of whatever had grabbed the bait on the other end.

The manically spinning reel slowed for a moment as the fish changed direction.

'Grab the reel' shouted Lizzie' Ben immediately complied holding rod and reel tightly in both hands and giving a heave on the taught line. He felt the weight of something large on the other end.

'I've got a fish' he shouted with a mixture of surprise, uncertainty and elation, but the fish had other ideas as it pulled hard on the line and tried to race away. Not really sure what to do he pulled against it. This nearly left him face down in water, but fortunately Lizzie steadied him as he overbalanced.

'Thanks' he said as he involuntarily loosened his grip on the reel, as the large fish thrashing its muscular tail headed out into the middle of the lake. Next time it slowed he grabbed the reel tightly in his left hand and the rod in his right. He jammed the base of the rod uncomfortably into his crotch to give him a better purchase. With Lizzie holding the rod higher up they both pulled hard.

'Wind in some of the line before it goes tight again' she shouted. This activity continued for some 10 minutes. They were getting tired but slowly they realized they were winning. The fish was tiring more quickly than they were.

'I can see it' Lizzie shouted. 'It must be over a foot long! Perhaps this is the Monster of Broad Oak'. The weakening fish was now about 10 feet away from them and close to the surface. It was spent and would be easy to land.

Ben was thinking how much he would enjoy showing this one to old Charlie, when in the corner of his eye he caught sight of a movement. Something very large was closing in on the thrashing fish attached to Ben's hook.

What happened next defied belief. In fact both children would have trouble sleeping at night for several weeks. The movement took on the shape, size and speed of a torpedo as it came into full view.

What they were looking at was the biggest fish they had ever seen. In an instant it opened its enormous gaping mouth, lined with rows of sharp backward pointing teeth and swallowed the near lifeless fish, hook, line and sinker. In the space of just a fraction of a second it had closed its mouth, turned and dived for deeper water, pulling the fishing line with it.

Ben gave a shout as the reel slipped out of his grip, the hard fought for line whipping away across the lake. As the reel unwound, Ben instinctively gripped the rod and bent his knees in anticipation.

When the final tug came Ben was caught completely unawares by its ferocity. A split second later he was surrounded by darkness as dirty water entered his mouth and nose.

Lizzie stood open-mouthed as the events unfolded. The whole episode probably only took five seconds with the grand finale being the sight of Ben dragged head first into the lake, with the rod skiding across the surface after the fast disappearing monster.

'Ben' she shouted in a mixture of dismay and terror. A second later he surfaced gasping and coughing water, bits of pond weed and small invertebrates back into the lake. Fortunately he was a fair swimmer and had had the sense to do what his dad always told him when working near water - he was wearing a life jacket. The self-inflating jacket had stopped him falling too deeply into the water, as he bobbed uncomfortably but safe on the lake surface.

Stretching out one of the special rescue poles, Lizzie was able to help a rather wet and visibly shaken Ben onto the bank.

There was no sign of the giant pike or any of the rod, line or fish it had plundered from them seconds earlier.

Neither of them spoke for a full minute. They just stared at each other. It was Lizzie who finally broke the silence.

'No one will believe us if we tell them' she said as she helped Ben to his feet, collected up the rest of their things and escorted a very wet and very smelly teenager homewards.

She was of course right. A thirteen-year-old boy and his best friend can cook up some interesting excuses between them to cover up the loss of a fishing rod and the real reason for a small boy returning home very wet and smelly.

Chapter Eleven
Mr. Angry to the Rescue

The seasons had moved on, with the summer holiday period drawing close, as August loomed. Sebastian and Sarah's cygnets were growing daily and becoming increasingly independent. Now close to half their parent's size they were less easy prey to the threat of mink or the giant pike that rumour had it lurked in the lake shallows.

It was a pleasant day, as Ben stood in the deep shade of the big old willow trees overhanging Eastern Lake. The cygnets were well away from their parents gobbling up the mass of duckweed that often gathered in this area of the lakes.

As Ben watched them he heard a distinct click and then a small splash of water. The splash was close to the cygnets, who all turned to see if some tit-bit had fallen into the water. A second crack followed, with a splash appearing closer to the cygnets. This time they were less happy with matters and made startled cheeps to their parent's. Sarah gave a sharp call and the cygnets paddled hurriedly towards her. A third crack and a splash rising up just behind the retreating cygnets confirmed Ben's fears. Someone was shooting at the birds from the cover of the trees. This was not the first time he had encountered an air-gun.

With a mixture of indignation and adrenalin-induced fear, Ben stood up and shouted 'Hoi stop that' at whoever it was. From out of the overhanging tree cover there came a cackling laugh, followed a few seconds later by a fourth crack of gunfire and the sound of an air-gun pellet as it ricocheted off one of the old willows behind him.

'Hey, stop it!'

Moments later 3 youths, perhaps a year older than himself, stepped out and walked in his direction. He immediately recognized them as Josh and his pals from St Vincent's and his heart sank. 'Who you talking to kid?' called Josh. 'Mr. Bigshot is he?' said the smaller of his two mates behind him. The third member of the gang was the biggest and potentially most intimidating, but looked a bit uncertain of himself. He joined in nonetheless 'What you goin' to do about it shrimp?'

As the three menacing figures advanced towards him, Ben felt the same surge of fear he had experienced during the race, when they had tried to get him. Once again he had an urge to run. An empty feeling suddenly appeared in the pit of his stomach and he felt the blood draining from his face. He felt cold. There were three of them; they were older than him, whilst Josh, the obvious leader of the group was waving his air-gun tauntingly. Looking around him Ben realized that running was not an option, he was cut off by the lake on three sides with the only way out blocked by the three advancing figures. Josh, slightly taller than Ben, with close-cropped hair under his baseball cap, had the air of one who knows he has control of a situation. The power of having two friends with him and the feel of a weapon in his hands gave him a rush of pleasure that he could not have resisted if he had wanted to. This was the kind of person capable of tormenting any weaker animal or person just for fun.

The smaller boy behind him looked a little younger and was probably close in age to Ben. He walked in that rather exaggerated fashion that said 'Look at me I'm special'. However as they came closer Ben could see uncertainty in the boy's eyes as they darted around him.

The third, much bigger boy now looked far less threatening as they approached. He had the round-shouldered stoop of someone who has always felt a bit of a freak amongst his much shorter contempories. His hair was unfashionably long and lank, being almost girl like. Ben assumed he was just a follower of the other two and posed little threat on his own.

A loner for much of his life, Ben had developed his own sense of values and was not one to follow the mainstream in order to conform, or to curry favour with others.

As Josh waived his air gun at him, Ben felt a rush of indignation at the situation. He hated bullies or anything that smacked of unfairness. Here he was, faced by people who felt they had him, and the wildlife of the reserve, at their mercy. He felt the anger rise up inside him, pushing aside his feelings of fear and self-preservation. He was just about to rush at the gang regardless of the outcome, when off to his left there came a crashing in the vegetation and a terrible ranting scream that Ben had heard once before.

On that occasion Ben had come close to wetting himself. This time the shock was far less, as out from the undergrowth stumbled the disheveled figure of Mr. Angry, whirling his shopping bags at the brambles and nettles that blocked his path up from the river. As ever he was screaming at the world with that same wild look in his eyes he had worn the last time they met.

This time however, it was not Ben who was most alarmed but the three figures in front of him. The bigger boy just turned and ran, without a second's thought, as he did Ben noticed a wet patch around his groin. Someone's mother was going to be asking questions of him later!

Ben saw his chance and ran at Josh, who was still staring open mouthed at Mr. Angry. Catching sight of Ben rushing at him, he turned in anticipation of a fight. However, the adjustment necessary to turn quickly towards Ben left him slightly off-balance. Ben caught him low at stomach height with all his weight. This was enough to cause the boy to over balance, but also caused Ben to ricochet at an angle towards the second, smaller boy.

As Josh caught his balance and shouted abuse at Ben, the adrenalin drove Ben's legs hard into the smaller boy, knocking him sideways. As he shifted his feet to keep his balance, the boy placed one into the thick sedge covered mud at the edge of the lake. For an instant it looked like the boy was going to end up in the water. Fortunately, or unfortunately for him he twisted his body to try to correct his fall. The mud held his right leg in a vice like grip, causing the twisting boy to end up face down in the thick black smelly mud at the edge of the lake.

Seeing his chance to escape Ben scuttled off in the direction the bigger boy had taken a few seconds earlier. As the lanky boy shot off left towards the river, Ben took the right hand fork towards Troll's Bridge and freedom. As he ran he risked a look over his right shoulder and caught site of Josh leveling his air gun at him. As the shot rang out, Ben ducked just in time to hear the pellet whiz over his head and bounce off the Troll's Bridge name sign.

Not wishing to chance a further pellet he continued running, until at a safe distance he looked back to see Josh helping his mud covered mate out of the lake margins. There was now no sign of the third boy, who was probably halfway to Sturry by now.

Slowing to walking pace Ben wondered what he should do next. The incident had left him well shaken, but more importantly he was thinking about the cygnets and other wildlife on the reserve and the prospect of those boys hurting them. He wondered should he report the matter, but another voice inside his head told him he shouldn't 'dob' on other kids. He realized how ridiculous this voice was and resolved to tell his dad about what had happened.

He found his father in the tool container gathering

materials together to prune branches overhanging the reserves footpaths. As ever his father greeted him with his trademark grin. When Ben explained what had happened his grin faded rapidly. His father was obviously very angry about the incident and the idea of anyone walking freely around the reserve with an air gun. He immediately rang the police and then belatedly thanked Ben for his initiative.

An hour later a police constable arrived at the nature reserve office with the three lads in tow. Ben was able to see them from the cover of his dad's office as the boys waited crestfallen in the waiting area in the adjacent conservatory.

The door opened and in stepped his dad and the constable.

'This is my son Ben, it was him who notified me about the air gun incident' said his dad.

'Hi' said the policeman as he pointed out of the window at the boys. 'Are those the young villain's in question?'

'Yes those are the ones' he replied a little nervously, recalling his earlier encounter with them.

'Ok, thank you very much young man. I'll be taking them round to their parents to report the matter'

'What will happen to them' said Ben.

'Not a lot,' He replied 'just a ticking off and maybe a caution. We'll be confiscating their air gun though.

Hopefully they won't try it on again, but if you have any further trouble with these three, or anyone else, be sure to let me know. Oh and well done. A lot of kids of your age wouldn't have the guts to bring it to the attention of the police, but unless we are told about incidents like this, there is nothing we can do to protect wildlife.'

Then he and Ben's father went to talk grim faced to the youngsters, before escorting them back to the police car. Ben hoped it would be the last he would see of them. At least they now knew he was not afraid to report them to the police and hopefully they would think twice before crossing swords with him again.

Chapter Twelve
The French Connection

The small boy staring into the clear lake water from Stinky Bridge presented a forlorn figure. How many of us visiting a foreign country, away from loved ones, surrounded by people with a different culture, find ourselves staring into water and are transported away, perhaps back to our home? Well on this sunny summers day in July, Canterbury was just such a place and the forlorn figure staring into the clear Broad Oak Lake waters, was just such a person.

****

Ben was helping his father on this sunny Saturday afternoon, by serving teas and selling souvenirs to the many visitors who had paid to visit the nature reserve. This was one of many ideas his father had come up with to rescue the nature reserve after the announcement of financial cuts earlier in the year. It was apparent to Ben that his father was becoming increasingly concerned about finding ways to raise the necessary money to get Creamer off his back.

His dad was also becoming increasingly irritable at home. All he seemed to have time for was his work, especially making money for the centre. It was becoming his obsession and whilst Ben wanted to help save it from those small-minded people who saw it just in terms of money, mostly he wanted his dad and the rest of the family to be happy.

Dad had come up with a variety of ideas, but opening the reserve to the general public at weekends, was one of his better ones.

Over a hundred people had visited that day, paying their entry fee, enjoying the sunshine, and buying refreshments after a pleasant walk around the areas open to the public. Now, as the day drew on towards closing time, Ben was free to explore.

His father had asked him to watch out for any lost visitors as he walked the trails around the lake and to point them back to the visitor centre before the reserve closed.

Taking his usual route he crossed Pegasus Bridge and stopped at Cygnet Point. No sign of swans or giant pike today. Next he cut along Reed Bed Walk and past Frog Pond, before coming to his favouritely named Stinky Bridge. It was here that he came upon the small, slender figure standing alone staring into the water.

'Hi' said Ben, keen to be friendly, 'What you doing here all on your own?'

The figure half turned to face him, with a slightly

startled look on his face. For a moment Ben was unsure whether he was talking to a boy or a girl. He was not very tall, with straight fair-coloured hair, which was rather on the long side for a boy. This, coupled with the delicate, elfin-like features and slight figure of the stranger, genuinely confused Ben. He always found girls hard to talk to, except Lizzie of course, but then she was different.

So assuming the stranger to be a girl he did his usual thing and blurted out something inappropriate. 'What's your name?'

'Pat' said the stranger in a foreign accent. 'My name Pat.'

Ben was still no nearer guessing whether the visitor was a boy or a girl, but he could hardly ask.

'Mama et Papa call me Patreek.' The boy continued in an accent he now assumed to be French. Ben involuntarily breathed a sigh of relief and warmed to the idea of making a new friend, now that he realized he was actually talking to a boy.

'Hi Pat' he offered half apologetically, 'my name's Ben. Are you French?'

'Oui' replied Pat. 'excusez moi ma English, but it is not good'

'My French is pretty naff too' comforted Ben

The French boy obviously hadn't understood him.

He decided to repeat in the kind of simple English his father used when talking to overseas visitors to the nature reserve, raising his voice as he did.

'Ma Francais pre-ttee bad' he said, pointing to his chest.

'You English pre-ttee bad too' repeated Pat, mimicking Ben's tone and volume perfectly. 'an zere iz no need to shout'

'Sorry' said Ben, taken aback 'I thought you didn't understand what I said'

'I understand much English, if you speak slow. But what does 'Naff' mean?'

'Oh, I see,' laughed Ben 'they probably don't teach you slang at school. Naff means not very good'

'Naff. I like that word. Perhaps you can teach me some more words like that?' said Pat.

'You bet' said Ben enthusiastically, thinking of all the words he knew, words that his parents would not like to hear him repeating'

'My aunty is called Pat' said Ben 'I can't call you the same name as her. She's a woman, and anyway she's got a moustache and smells of mint imperials all the time'

Pat laughed loudly at this description.

'What is mint imperial?' Asked Pat.

'I don't know. Some kind of sweet, bon-bons. It's just something my dad says about her. Anyway I can't call you Pat, so I'll call you Paddy from now on. OK?' He added.

'Paddy?' the French boy repeated, pointing to his chest. 'Yes, Paddy is good, I like that. And what will I call you?' The French boy paused for a second as though considering the options. 'I theeenk....... Ben, because it is your name.'

Both boys laughed nervously at Paddy's humour, which helped overcome the embarrassment of their introduction and made them feel more at ease with each other.

'Good.' Agreed Ben. 'Would you like me to show you round the nature reserve?'

Paddy appeared to understand, nodding and smiling in approval.

As they walked, they tried hard to understand each other in a strange mix of English and French. As with all small children the world over, language was not so much of a problem, as long as you could point at things and laugh about them. Ben felt important and responsible showing this unexpected foreign guest around 'his' reserve, pointing out plants and animals and listening to Paddy repeat the words. In his turn Paddy would try to give the name in French.

Eventually they came to the Kingfisher Hide where they could sit quietly and look out over the lake.

'What are you here for' said Ben 'Why are you in England?'

' I am staying with my mother for les vacances – err, holidays' he corrected himself ' My mother is visiting the university for the summer. My sister is with us, she is fifty years old, I think'

'Fifteen, I think' corrected Ben, laughing at the thought of Paddy having a fifty year old sister. 'Quinz?'

Yes fifteen years and I am thirteen I think'

'Treize' added Ben, whilst Paddy agreed smiling.

'Same age as me.'

They both laughed nervously at the coincidence.

'We want something do today, so Valentine and Maman bring me here, see.' He added with difficulty. 'They want sit and talk. I want er …. explore'.

Then Ben remembered that his job was to make sure none of the visitors was still on the reserve. So they both hurried around the lake until they came to the Long Bridge. Then they heard a woman's voice coming from the direction of Pylon Picnic Site, calling Paddy's name.

'Ici Maman,' called Paddy.

'Ah Patreeck, tu est la.' She chided him slightly, 'Oh you have a friend' she added in near perfect English.

'Hello, have you been playing together?' she said to Ben.

A little bashfully Ben said. 'Yes, we have been watching the Kingfishers and I have been showing Paddy round the nature reserve'

'Paddy? Is that what you call my son? I like that. You must be very good friends already. What name should we call you by?' she asked smiling in that animated manner that the French like to use.

'Hi - I'm Ben'

'Hello, I'm Astrid, Astrid Davidson and this is my daughter Valentine,' indicating towards her daughter, 'We are on holiday here for the summer. I am really here to work, at the University, so Valentine and Patrick are actually the ones on holiday.'

Valentine smiled and nodded.

'Patrick's father is back in Nice, where we live. He's English.' She added, revealing another interesting fact about Paddy.

'Do you live in Canterbury Ben?' She enquired.

'Yes I do.' He replied politely. Ben immediately liked Mrs. Davidson, who seemed so genuine with her shock of wild, curly blonde hair and her ready smile.

'Actually my Dad looks after the nature reserve here.' He informed her, feeling a twinge of self-importance at revealing the fact. 'Do you think Paddy would like to play here with me one day?'

'I'm sure he'd love to. And I'm sure Valentine would welcome any chance not to have to look after him, whilst I'm busy at the university, wouldn't you Valentine?' she said turning to the tall blonde teenager next to her.

'You bet' She replied, also without a trace of a French accent. 'Then I can visit the shops with my English friends'

'Would your father mind? Perhaps we should ask him first?' added Mrs. Davidson.

'No he'd be delighted' came the voice of his father, as he approached from the direction of the education centre. 'Hello, I'm Will Franklin, Dad.' And the two adults shook hands. 'Ben could use someone to keep him occupied over the summer holidays. He gets bored on his own. In fact we are having a family barbecue down here tomorrow, would you all like to come for lunch?'

That was what Ben liked about his father, always inviting total strangers to look around his precious nature reserve.

Ben and Paddy smiled at each other. All of a sudden Ben felt the summer holidays wouldn't be so bad after all.

Chapter Thirteen
A New Deal

'Hi' came the voice of Jackie over the phone. Jackie was the New Deal supervisor from City Hall. 'I'm sending a new chap down today. 'He's just come onto our books. If we can start him today, then that would be great.'

'What's his background 'said Dad.

'He lives locally, but I think he's a bit of a nomad. He seems to have been around, doing various jobs, mostly building'. She replied 'Anyway if you think he's ok you can get him started and at the same time take the money due to you.'

The New Deal scheme was another of Dad's little earners. For every New Deal placement he took on to give work experience to, the nature reserve received a fee.

'OK send him along. We certainly need the money and with a bit of luck he will have some useful skills we can use.' Then he added 'What's his name?'

'You know' said Jackie 'It's most odd, but I don't seem to have all his paper-work here, although I do recall his name as being Alan.'

****

In Pond Lab Ben and Paddy were busy looking in their large white trays trying to find as many water creatures as they could. They'd just popped outside between downpours to stir up the lake water with their pond nets and collect a few creatures.   As the rain started falling again they dashed back inside and put their catches on the tables of Pond Lab.

As they inspected their catch a familiar voice came from behind him.

'What have we caught today then? The Broad Oak Monster?'

Next to Dad was a small, dark-haired, dark-skinned man, with rather shifty unsmiling eyes. The presence of this scowling stranger somehow made Ben feel uncomfortable.

'This is my son Ben and his friend Paddy. Bonjour Paddy'.

'Bonjour Monsiour Franklin.'

'This is Alan.' He said, indicating his companion. 'He's going to be working with us for the next 3 months'

The unsmiling visitor gave the faintest of nods and said nothing.

'Right' said Dad to Alan. 'I guess I'd better introduce you to Charlie, the supervisor you'll be working with'.

'Keep up the good work boys' He said, as the two men turned and left.

'I not like that man.' Said Paddy. 'He look mean'

'Yes' Said Ben 'He looks like trouble to me too.'

****

Before too long the skies started to clear enough for Ben and Paddy to venture out onto the reserve. Ben had already told Paddy about his friend Peter the sculptor and Paddy was interested to see some of the work he had done.

After showing Paddy some of the fascinating sculptures created on the reserve, the two friends reached Knackers' Hole, where Peter was busily working on The Pylon Bird. Peter stopped his work, which involved being perched on top of a stepladder, screwing together the mass of wooden triangles that made up the bird's body. The head and neck were still to be completed, but it was already a formidable looking creature.

'This is Paddy.' Said Ben, indicating towards his friend. 'He's French'

'French?' Said Peter 'Bonjour Paddy. Comment allez vous?'

'Bonjour' Replied Paddy 'C'est un oiseux?'

The two then proceeded to chat away in French, with Ben looking on understanding snippets of information and being even more impressed with Peter. Was there no limit to his talents?

Everyone was really pleased with the way Peter's sculptures were starting to add interest to the natural magic of the reserve. Peter was fast becoming Ben's hero. He hoped that he would work on the reserve forever.

****

'Not seen my knife have you Ben?' Asked Peter a few day's later as Ben and Paddy each stood drinking a Fruit Shoot from the centre shop, looking into a large fish tank full of pond creatures.

'No' said Ben, 'It's not your best sharp one is it?'

'I'm afraid so' replied Peter, 'I'm sure I lent it to that new guy Alan, but he says he hasn't seen it.'

'I don't trust him.' Said Paddy. 'I think he is bad'

'You don't think he stole it do you?' Added Ben.

'I suppose he could have, but I don't think so. I probably just dropped it next to one of the sculptures. I'll just have to look for it.' He said resignedly.

Chapter Fourteen
Uneasy Times

With pressures heaped on his shoulders by Creamer and the decision-makers at City Hall, Dad rarely left his office and often worked well into the evening. The atmosphere at home was no longer the convivial one Ben recalled when his dad first started his job at Broad Oak Lakes.

Creamer was a not infrequent visitor to the reserve, constantly having meetings with his dad. When Creamer left these meetings, his dad always had a grim look on his face.

Making one of his regular visits to the nature reserve, Ben called into the office to say hello. Creamer was just leaving his Dad's office as he arrived.

'OK I'll be along next Wednesday to check on progress. Hopefully we will see an improvement on next terms bookings by then' Said Creamer and left without waiting for a reply.

'You OK Dad?' Said Ben, a worried look etched across his face.

'Yes son' He replied realizing that Ben was genuinely concerned.

'And thanks for asking. I'm sorry if I'm not being very good company these days, but it seems that more powerful people than me are determined to see this place closed. It's down to me to find a way of convincing the right people that it is worth keeping Broad Oak Lakes open.' Confided his dad.

'Of course it is. Why would anyone want to close it down?' Said Ben.

'Some of the bean counters at City Hall think they have put too many beans into this place. What they can't see, because they never leave their offices, is how many of those beans have flourished. I'm talking about the enormous number of children that have passed through this place over the years'

'So what can we do?' Enquired Ben.
'We can find ways of earning more money and convince as many important people as possible of our value' He replied. 'If Creamer was on our side it would make a big difference. All he seems to do is find fault and waste my valuable time with these pointless meetings'.

With that he returned to his office, to make more phone calls and write more letters, leaving Ben to ponder how he might help.

As he stepped out of the visitor centre buildings he noticed Creamer talking to Alan by the Sensory Shed.

They might have been discussing the amazing structure built by Charlie called 'The Water Cycle'.

This consisted of two children's bicycles linked together by an array of levers and chains. The whole contraption was powered by a steady stream of water pumped from the lake. Like some weird water-wheel, the water turned each of the wheels, cogs, levers and chains in sequence, with the end product being tinkling chimes and a small black spider rising and falling on its thread.

All the visiting children and adults to the nature reserve would stare enraptured by this mechanical folly. Somehow though he couldn't imagine that Creamer or Alan were capable of any such interest. Seeing these two together, talking in such a secretive way, fuelled Ben's suspicions that they were up to something. He decided to sneak up to where they were and attempt to listen in on their conversation. Using the cover of the trees between the Sensory Garden and the Water Cycle, Ben was able to get close enough to hear a few exchanged words. None of it made any sense to him, except the word substation. Why were these two discussing the substation he wondered?

Just then Charlie appeared at the door of the shed that he used as his workshop. Seeing Ben hiding behind the trees he shouted. 'Hello Ben. What you doin' there? Seen something interesting I'll bet.'

Immediately Creamer and Alan turned and looked at him suspiciously. 'What are you creeping around there for? Looking for one of your creepy crawly friends in the dirt are you? Or were you perhaps listening in on a private conversation.' Asked Creamer in his usual slightly sarcastic tone.

Ben bridled at the accusation 'No I wasn't' His face now a guilty red complexion.

'I was trying to find a woodlouse' He said a might unconvincingly.

'Goin' to give it to your friend Lizzie were you?' Winked Charlie, failing to pick up on the tension between Ben and Creamer. " 'Spect she would rather be given flowers. My missus certainly wouldn't have wanted woodlice when we was courtin" He added mischievously.

At this Ben went even redder, turned away from the gathered adults and strutted off to lick his wounds on Teddy Bear Island. As he sat on a tree stump, his indignation still simmering, he heard the sound of someone pushing a wheelbarrow in the direction of the Swamp Path. Through the trees Ben caught a fleeting glimpse of Alan, pushing the wheelbarrow along the track. Ben was suspicious of everything Alan did, especially after seeing him apparently conspiring with Creamer. Then there was Peter's missing knife. Ben decided to follow him.

He was able to follow Alan at quite a distance, owing to the racket his wheelbarrow made. He didn't want to get too close. Following the noise, Ben made his way along the lakeshore for several minutes, until the noise stopped suddenly. Ben moved more cautiously now until he heard a splashing sound ahead. He very carefully made his way along one of the many fingers of land that projected into the lake until he was able to see Alan further along, dipping a long stick in the water.

At first Ben assumed he was 'pond dipping' with a fishing net, but on second thoughts he realized this was not the sort of thing a miserable individual like Alan would do. Then the long handle was lifted high above Alan's head, revealing a long handled rake-like tool. It was a crome, a tool that looks a bit like a pitch-fork, with long bent teeth at one end. The staff often used tools such as this for dragging unwanted weed out of ponds around the reserve. Alan was fishing, but what for wondered Ben?

Moving a little further along the finger of land, Ben was able to get a clearer view of proceedings. He was now able to see that Alan was in the process of dragging a large black plastic sack from the lake.

Alan opened the top of the bag and peered at its contents. Apparently satisfied with what he found inside, he heaved the bag into the wheelbarrow and headed off towards the river bank.

Ben had to creep quietly back up the finger of land he was on and then follow the noise of the wheelbarrow.

As he reached Canterbury Woods the clattering of the wheel barrow stopped. Ben guessed that Alan was probably by the Willow Close Gate, which led onto the riverbank next to the reserve. Rather than risk running into Alan on the path, he cut off through the woods and out through a hole in the fence he knew about. This brought him onto the river bank about 50 metres from the gate.

From the cover of the trees he was able to see Alan talking to someone by the riverbank. He was also just able to hear their voices. He recognized Alan's voice, but the voice of the man he was talking to was not familiar. It was not one of the nature reserve staff.

He decided to risk creeping a little closer, being careful not to stand on any dead twigs as he did so. Eventually he was only about 30 metres from the two men. Alan was talking to a swarthy skinned man, with hair as dark as Alan's. He was a big man, with a distinctive butterfly-shaped scar under his right eye. He had the look of a gypsy about him and Ben suspected he was the kind of individual capable of getting into a fight at the drop of a hat.

Ben was able to pick up the words 'boat' and 'wheels'. The other man seemed to be indicating downstream. Ben got the distinct impression this man was negotiating with Alan. He was standing facing Scarface, with his arms folded across his chest. Occasionally he would hold his right hand up to his face to rest his chin on, or would rub his mouth as they spoke. The topic of discussion appeared contentious, with Scarface frequently becoming agitated, thumping his right fist into the open palm of his other hand, suggesting he was being forceful in his demands. Evidently the two men were not in total agreement about matters.

Eventually their discussion appeared to come to a conclusion. It was then that Ben noticed the black plastic sack standing between the two men, its top apparently opened up for inspection. At the end of their meeting

Scarface bent down, quickly fastened the top of the sack and swung it effortlessly onto his shoulder.

Alan turned to collect the wheelbarrow and quickly disappeared back through the gate. He could hear the clattering of the empty barrow as he trundled it along Jungle Walk, towards Kingfisher Hide.

As Scarface marched past Ben, with the black plastic sack on his shoulder, Ben crouched down in the undergrowth so that he wouldn't be seen. As the big gypsy strode away, Ben relaxed and let out a slow breath. Then as he looked back to where the meeting had taken place, Ben spotted a small white Jack Russell Terrier sniffing about amongst the brambles growing along the riverbank. The big gypsy stopped and shouted something to the dog and it immediately obeyed, trotting after its master.

As the dog drew level with Ben it paused and sniffed the air. Ben tried to keep as still as possible for fear that the dog might give him away. Suddenly the dog gave a low growl, followed by a short bark.

'Shhh.' Said Ben, in the hope that the dog might do as he asked.

Instead the dog broke out into a mixture of short yaps and low growls as it bounced stiff legged, backwards and forwards, not 3 metres from the greatly alarmed Ben hiding in the bushes.

Scarface stopped again and shouted something at the dog, which momentarily stopped its barking. But the temptation to bark at Ben was just too much for it. Once again Ben found himself at risk of being given away by this wretched little creature.

'Get over here you stupid animal!' Bellowed Scarface, as he put the sack on the ground and advanced towards the barking dog and the poorly concealed Ben.

Once again Ben found himself wondering whether to run or remain hidden from someone he had been spying on. However, the dog made the decision for him, deciding that the hidden Ben was not worth his master's wrath. It scuttled off along the path towards its master wagging its tail in an attempt to seek his favour. As it scuttled past Scarface he swung a large heavy boot in its direction, which it only just managed to avoid.

To Ben's relief, man and dog both disappeared from view, leaving the shaken Ben squatting in the undergrowth, thankful not to have been confronted by this new and threatening character, who seemed to be taking an interest in the nature reserve.

Once the danger had passed, Ben found himself wondering what the two men had been talking about and what was in the black plastic sack that Alan had taken from the lake. It was only then that he made the connection between the activities he had just witnessed and what Old Danny had told him a few weeks earlier, about thefts from the builders' merchants.

Was the sack full of stolen goods perhaps? Were Alan and Scarface involved? And was there possibly a connection with Creamer? Ben's imagination caught fire.

Whatever it was, the suspicious activities of so many strangers suggested something significant was happening at Broad Oak Lakes. Ben just wondered what it could possibly be?

Chapter Fifteen
Scarface

The gypsy picked his way up through the gap in the barbed-wire fence between the river and the nature reserve. He was an easy man to recognise at well over 6 feet tall, with huge shoulders, a dark complexion and a mop of jet-black hair. The most distinctive feature about him, should you ever have the misfortune to make his acquaintance, was the butterfly shaped scar he bore beneath his right eye socket. The scar gave him the sort of aggressive look that many 'tough' young men aspire to. Scarface was as vicious and ugly on the inside as he looked on the outside.

Behind him, trotting at his heels, was the Jack Russell terrier that Ben had encountered a few days earlier. It was in fact probably the thinnest looking Jack Russell you are ever likely to set eyes on. Scarface often bragged to his fellow ne'r-do-wells, that he kept the poor dog half starved to keep it vicious. A trait he considered useful in a dog bred for badger baiting. He was aware that there were no badgers on the nature reserve, but he was here on other business.

As he picked his way up through the trees of Stour View Woods, he quickly topped the rise at Electric Avenue, where he came to a sudden halt. From this vantage point he was able to view the whole of the 400Kv substation below. The dog walked close behind his master, sniffing the ground for interesting doggy smells. This was doggy heaven, with the essence of every conceivable animal a Jack Russell might wish to pursue. In fact so distracted was he by the new smells that he picked up, that he didn't realize his master had stopped, until he ran clean into the back of his legs.

'Stupid animal!' Cursed the ill-tempered gypsy and placed a well-aimed kick at the unfortunate creature. As the heavy steel toe-capped boot made contact with the end of the dog's nose, it let out a yelp of pain and scuttled off down the track, its short and rather mangy looking tail held tight between its legs.

'Get lost, you stupid mut' Cursed Scarface. The dog sensed that this was not a time to be around his bad tempered master and after pausing briefly to double check on the situation, he trotted off towards Butterfly Bank.

'You'll be back' He spat, as the dog shambled off into the distance, intent on exploring the cocktail of smells the nature reserve presented.

Scarface turned his attention back to the substation for a few seconds, before coming to a decision, whereupon he made a bee-line for the section of fence between The Amphitheatre and Marsh Orchid Mere.

A few minutes later he was standing facing his chosen

section of fence, paying particular attention to the pebbles on the ground beneath it. Next he swung the backpack off his shoulders and onto the ground in front of him. From out of the top of the pack, he pulled a short handled trenching tool, similar to those commonly found in army surplus stores.

Next he proceeded to dig at the mass of pebbles that extended across the whole of the substation compound floor, including up to half a metre beyond the electrified boundary fence.

Within a few minutes he was able to excavate enough pebbles to make a trench deep enough for a man to wriggle under the electrified wires that were placed just a few centimetres beyond the mesh fencing. Then, satisfied with what he had achieved, he back-filled the trench until it was almost impossible to detect any sign of his digging whatsoever. Next he tied a short length of orange baler twine to the fence, before returning along the made-up path from Rock Down to Electric Avenue.

'Where's that bloody dog' He muttered under his breath 'I'll kill the bloody thing once I get my hands on it'. With his temper still simmering he marched off down the path along which the dog had scuttled several minutes earlier.

****

Whilst the gypsy was scouting around the 400 Kv substation, the bruised and perpetually hungry Jack

Russell was trotting down the muddy track from Butterfly Bank to Eastern Lake.

He stopped on one occasion to sniff hopefully at a fox scat, but decided the fox's droppings held little of interest, even to the hungriest of hounds.

Eventually he found himself at the shore of Eastern Lake, which appeared to offer a much better prospect of finding something to eat.

****

The young otter had been swimming up the River Stour for several hours from its regular haunt at Sturry. Chased off by parent's jealous to guard their territory, it had taken the hint and spent some considerable time exploring a stretch of river with no recent signs of other otters, although plenty of human smells, of which it was wary.

Eventually it found itself in the stretch of river between the ASDA supermarket on one side and a promising area of trees on the other. Climbing up the steep sides of the river bank it sniffed around the bank-side vegetation for any suitable hole or cleft in tree roots, for it to adopt as a holt.

The large black plastic pipe put in place by Charlie and a number of local wildlife volunteers, was just what it was looking for. Dad had hoped that this bit of conservation work might entice any passing otters into the reserve. Had he been able to watch the events taking place, he would have been delighted. The pipe led under the nature reserve fence, opening out next to Eastern Lake. The otter slowly sniffed its way along the strange tunnel, emerging into the daylight on the other side a minute later.

As the young otter emerged from the pipe, it sniffed the air carefully, picking up the scent of the nearby lake. Satisfied that all was well, it headed in the direction of the water and the prospect of a rewarding afternoon's fishing.

****

The Jack Russell stood stock still, listening. Something was moving through the vegetation at the side of the path. Ears pricked, its whole body was rigid in anticipation. Next second a strange creature, little smaller than itself, appeared from the path-side vegetation. As it paused on the path, it looked straight at the watching dog. Both creatures stared at each other for a second or two, each wondering what to do. However, the young otter 'blinked first'. Turning away from the Jack Russell, it bolted for the relative safety of the water nearby.

This was all the encouragement the near rigid dog needed. As the otter shot away, he sprang into action, barking madly as he gave chase. With a splash the otter launched itself into the murky waters of the lake, scattering the group of cygnets busily dabbling in the lake shallows. Hot on its trail, the Jack Russell stopped just short of the water, but continued to bark wildly at the receding wave of the disappearing otter.

The excitement of the chase was just too much for the dog, which now began to bark at the lake, marching up and down and showing its indignation to the world. The young swans, initially spooked by the otter, swam to the protection of their mother, Sarah, expressing their concerns through high-pitched cheeping.

With the otter now gone, the Jack Russell turned its attention on the retreating figures of the cygnets. Suddenly the whole air filled with the sound of powerful beating wings. As the dog turned in the direction of the noise, the last thing it saw was a mass of white feathers as a large white bird descended upon it.

****

Sebastian had been by the far bank of the lake when the dog first appeared. He watched it for a while, wary of any threat it might pose to his offspring. He had never encountered a dog before, as they were not allowed on site. He watched as the other strange animal appeared. It looked a little like the mink that were such a threat to his family when they were still young. Even as big as they were now, Sebastian was still protective towards them in the face of the threat a mink presented.

However it was once the dog started barking that Sebastian was at his most alarmed. As the cygnets bolted for the cover of their mother, he launched himself into the air in the direction of the dog. As his powerful wings struck the dog across the head, the dog immediately stopped barking and was knocked headlong into the murky waters of the lake.

As it floated motionless in the water, the dog showed no signs of life, its face below the lake surface. Satisfied that the danger from the dog was over Sebastian swam over to where Sarah was making concerned bleating noises as she fussed around her cygnets. The mink-like creature appeared to have disappeared now, but Sebastian decided to lead his family away from any danger, heading in the direction of Trolls Bridge, leaving the still, lifeless body of the dog floating on the surface of the lake.

****

Up at Electric Avenue Scarface was busy cursing his dog when he heard its mad barking coming from the direction of the lakes.

'Stupid Animal' He cursed again. 'Bloody thing! Last thing I want is for someone to spot me here. I'll kill it!' And he ran off along the path in the direction of the barking dog.

A few seconds later, the barking suddenly stopped. With a mixture of relief and suspicion he continued running down the track past Butterfly Bank until he came to the shore of Eastern Lake. He could see no sign of the dog, just a family of swans as they swam away from him.

Then a few metres away from the bank he spotted

something white floating in the lake. It was his dog. There was no doubt in his mind that it had drowned in the lake.

'Stupid mut!' He mumbled to himself. 'Bloody thing couldn't even swim. Still with what I'm set to make from this job, there'll be plenty left to get me a new one.'

Without an ounce of remorse he turned and headed back up the track, the fate of the dog now the last thing on his mind.

Chapter Sixteen
The Headless Dog

It was yet another blistering day in August. Ben, Lizzie and Paddy were sitting dangling their bare feet off the jetty and into the cool clear water of the lake. Paddy noticed that some of the waterweed floating on the lake surface had small yellow flowers growing out above the water surface.

'What is that little yellow flower' enquired Paddy, pointing at the mass of yellow flowers, poking out of the water on their tiny stalks.

'Oh they're killers!' said Lizzie dramatically.

'Do you mean they're poisonous?' chipped in Ben.

'No, worse than that. They're carnivorous'

'Sacre bleu' whistled Paddy; quickly lifting his feet out of the water 'You mean they attack us?'

'No' Laughed Lizzie. 'They trap tiny creatures called water-fleas. Then they slowly digest them. They are not dangerous to humans'.

'I've got an idea' Said Ben 'How's about we take Conker out and give Paddy a closer look at the vicious world of the underwater jungle?'

Conker was the nature reserve's wooden boat.

'Sounds good to me' Said Lizzie 'But we'll need to wear life jackets and make sure your Dad knows where we've gone in the boat.'

'Of course' Agreed Ben 'I've got my mobile phone as well, in case we have any problems. You fancy coming Paddy?'

'What ho' Said Paddy in a mock English accent, that had them all falling about laughing.

Ben dashed in to the visitor centre office and found his Dad bent over a computer screen.

'Dad, would it be OK to take Conker out on the lake? We'll wear life jackets and I've got my mobile with me' asked Ben.

'I reckon you are sensible enough to manage that, as long as you are all going. Which part of the lake are you off to?' enquired Dad.

'Great! We'll go to Eastern Lake.'

'That's quite a distance. Still at least I know where to go looking for your remains if the Troll gets you' He joked.

'Thanks Dad' Said Ben as he disappeared through the door.

After getting his Dad's approval, Ben, Lizzie and Paddy set about getting together all their needs. Ben fetched the electric outboard motor and battery, whilst Lizzie fetched all the pond-dipping equipment. Paddy gave Ben a hand, transporting life jackets. Ben clamped the outboard onto the boats stern and fitted the battery in place. The bilges of the boat needed to have water pumped out of them because the boat had a slow leak. Being a clinker-built boat, the curved strips of overlapping wood forming its hull did not form a perfect seal. Small amounts of water seeped in and pooled in the bottom of the boat. They decided to take a small bucket with them to bale out any water that came in during their voyage.

When they had all they needed, the three children climbed carefully into the boat, each enveloped in a rather large lifejacket. Paddy sat at the bow end, with Lizzie midway down the boat and Ben at the stern, controlling the direction of travel using the tiller, which was connected by a vertical pole to the spinning blade of the electric outboard. Twisting the tiller grip clockwise increased the speed of the boat, whilst twisting it anticlockwise slowed the boat, or even put it into reverse. Ben had completed his training using the outboard and was well aware of the dangers that even such a low powered motor posed if not handled with care.

Ben guided the boat across the lakes to the narrow passage at Troll's Bridge. With a little help from the other two, pulling on reeds or pushing an oar into the lake bed, Ben was able to negotiate the passage.

Beyond Troll's Bridge they found themselves moving through a sea of green as the boat pushed its way through a carpet of tiny floating leaves.

'Duck weed', advised Lizzie. 'It often collects in Eastern Lake during hot summers.'

Paddy dunked his hands through the duckweed, parting it in front of the slow moving boat. 'I clear path' he shouted.

As his hands pushed the weed aside, his fingers brushed against something large, cold and firm under the water.

'I think I have stick!' he shouted as his hand closed around a long thin branch-like projection. As he pulled the stick he realized it was attached to a larger object, which he took for an old wet tree trunk. He shifted his position in the bow of the boat, intent on pulling the object out to show his friends. Standing in the bow of the boat, with his left hand braced against the bow, he pulled hard.

'Be careful Paddy' Warned Lizzie fearing the worst.

As Paddy pulled hard the object rose out of the lake, covered in duckweed. As he lifted it he turned to show off his trophy to the others. It was only then that he caught wind of the fowl stench and he realized what he was holding. Gripped in his hand was the leg of a small dog, attached to it was the animal's bloated body. But the most horrifying part was the total absence of a head.

Screaming, Paddy dropped the dog's body. Unfortunately for him the action left him off balance. From the back of the boat Ben watched in horror as Paddy tipped over the front of the boat, his legs following as if in slow motion behind him.

Lizzie and Ben rushed to the front of the boat in time to witness the hapless Paddy bob back to the surface covered in a green coating of duckweed. He gasped for air and thrashed about him in panic, although the life jacket provided all the buoyancy he needed. In his panic he placed his hand on the dead dog's body, where its head should have been attached.

'Aaarrrggghhh' He cried pulling his hand away from it 'Sacre bleu! C'est un chien sans un tete. Aidez moi!'

His eyes were wide with terror as he grabbed the edge of the wooden boat, desperate to get out of the water. As he put his weight onto the boat's side, it lurched sideways, threatening to tip the whole boat, Ben and Lizzie included. Fortunately for them the wide bottomed boat was very stable. Ben and Lizzie were able to take an arm each and pull him struggling and screaming from the water. By grabbing hold of his jeans he was eventually landed, breathing heavily, into the bottom of the boat.

Once they had been able to calm the terrified French boy, who continued to utter a selection of words that neither Lizzie nor Ben had heard before, they were able to draw breath and take stock of the situation. As Ben and Lizzie looked at the bedraggled, forlorn figure sitting in the bow of the boat, Lizzie found it hard to stifle a giggle. As she fought to gain control of herself, Ben looked at her. He too started to giggle.

'Not funny!' said the soaking Paddy, his head sporting a soft green cap of duckweed. It was no good. Both Ben and Lizzie were now totally unable to control their laughter. Paddy looked at them both his mouth open wide in horror, that they should be laughing at him.

'Look at you' Roared Ben.

Realizing they might be hurting his feelings, Lizzie tried to comfort him. 'Sorry Paddy, it's not funny. But you look like Millie Green Fingers, the witch of the lake' and despite herself she continued to double up with laughter.

Paddy wiped the duckweed off his head and looked at the rest of his body covered in green slime. Very slowly the raucous laughter of his friends overcame the dismay and feelings of indignation he had felt at first. A smile cracked his dirty, slimy wet face, which turned to a giggle and then full-blown, uncontrollable laughter.

It took the children a good few minutes to regain control, before Ben had a sudden thought.

'What is a dead dog doing in the lake and what happened to its head?'

'Perhaps it fell in and drowned?' Suggested Lizzie

'A Troll?' added Ben, in his best horror movie tone.

'Or maybe Carnivorous Flowers?' Said Paddy with a deadpan face.

Lizzie and Ben looked at Paddy. All covered in green weed and looking for all-the-world like some kind of strange carnivorous plant himself, and they both started laughing again.

'Une Fleur Sauvage' Roared Lizzie pointing at Paddy and holding onto her stomach.

'Oh please stop'.

She and Ben were crying now, with the unfortunate Paddy forced to join in with them, roaring with laughter at his own expense.

'Well it certainly brings a whole new meaning to 'Wild Flowers'.' Added Ben, and they all started laughing again.

****

As they sat laughing in Conker, the family of swans quietly sat at the lake surface, helping themselves, with the aid of their long necks, to the weed on the bottom of the lake. Despite being free, the food was hard won. Every year Sarah and Sebastian raised their cygnets, with few surviving to adulthood thanks to the threat from foxes, pike and mink that inhabit the dark and savage world largely hidden from human eyes. Sebastian often had to chase off other swans, intent on moving into his lake-land territory. Even the cygnets that survived long enough to undergo the transformation from ugly duckling to white-feathered adults were in their turn chased off by Sebastian.

This year Sebastian had been very successful defending his family, with the cygnets growing particularly well as a result. The usual predators had come his way and he had been able to remain master of the lake. The intervention of the strange dog had been an unusual event, threatening the cygnets. He had dealt with that incident by charging the barking animal, wings flapping wildly and catching the dog with their full force and propelling it unconscious into the murky green waters of the lake.

Sebastian appeared well satisfied with his year's work, whilst his life partner Sarah contentedly moved amongst her cygnets looking as beautiful as ever.

No human eyes had witnessed what happened to the dog and how it came to be killed, only those of the lakes permanent residents. And how did it come to loose its head? Not even Sebastian was privy to that information, no-one and no-thing knew, except perhaps the owner of the dark malevolent eyes lying motionless at the bottom of the lake, watching and seeing everything!

Chapter Seventeen
A Close Shave

Ben, Paddy and Lizzie were sitting in their favourite hide-away at Energy Heights. The place Ben and Lizzie had first met on that rainy day in February.

This was an unusual day. Being a Sunday morning, Lizzie would usually be out at her riding lessons, whilst Paddy would normally be at church.

However, Paddy's Mum was laid up in bed with a tummy bug, whilst Paddy's sister Valentine was tasked with looking after her and cooking Sunday lunch.

Coincidentally Lizzie's riding instructor was also bed-ridden.

She had called round to see Ben quite early, to find Paddy already there. They were about to go to the nature reserve and indulge in a bit of bird spotting.

Lizzie decided to join them. So the three of them trooped off for a quiet Sunday morning at the reserve. The reserve was closed to the public on Sundays, so they'd have it all to themselves.

"Look' said Lizzie pointing across towards Buzz Bank.

'A kestrel,' she exclaimed, 'hovering over the long grass. Just beyond the transformers. Just outside the compound'.

'Oui' agreed Paddy "c'est un faucon'

"Is that what you call it in French?' asked Ben "It sounds like falcon. Sometimes we call birds of prey falcons.

"Yes' said Lizzie, 'whose knowledge seemed to know no limits "The Latin, or more correctly its scientific name, is Falco tinunculus. Watch how it hovers in the sky waiting to swoop on some unsuspecting creature'.

'What is swoop?' asked Paddy, always hungry to learn a new word.

'Fly - voile - very fast, down to the ground to catch a mouse or a vole'

'What is a vole?' Said Paddy continuing with his learning of English, undaunted by the task of having to learn so many new words at one go.

'I can answer that one' said Ben triumphantly. 'It's a small fury mammal, a bit like a mouse, but with short ears, a shorter tail and a rather chubby body.'

'Merci' Said Paddy. He trained his binoculars on the kestrel as it flapped its wings in such a manner that it could keep itself in the same position for long periods of time.

'Some people call it a 'wind hover', because of the way it seems to be held in one position like a kite on a string.' added Ben, making sure that Lizzie didn't get all the credit for having brains.

'Look' cried Paddy 'It is swoop'.

As his broken English indicated, the kestrel swooped down to the ground and a few seconds later it rose again with a small dark, furry object held in its talons. The bird then flew across the compound to alight on one of the concrete structures, where it would quickly set about eating its prey.

As they followed its flight Lizzie exclaimed "There's someone walking over there.'

'Where?' Said Ben. 'There shouldn't be anyone on the reserve this morning; it's closed to the public. I hope it's not those foul kids from the estate across the river. I don't want to cross swords with them again'

'No' Said Lizzie' it's not kids, it's two men walking along by the perimeter fence. Perhaps they're Grid maintenance men? I don't recognize either of them though'

'I recognize them' said Ben, once he'd got his binoculars focused on one of the men. 'That's the new guy from New Deal, that Paddy and I met last week. Alan. I don't like him much. Very shifty character. Didn't you think so Paddy?'

'Oui. I not like him much. Tres mal personne je pense.'

'The other one is Scarface.' He added.

'Scarface?' Quizzed Lizzie. 'How did he get that name?'

'I don't think it's his real name. I just call him that because he has a scar on his face. I saw him and Alan down by the riverbank together a few days ago. They looked like they were up to no good. I think he must be one of the gypsies Old Danny told us about. He had a pet Jack Russell Terrier with him. But there's no sign of it now.' Observed Ben.

'Qu'est ce que c'est?' Asked Paddy. 'Jack Russell Terrier. What is this?'

'A small white dog' Explained Lizzie 'Un petit chien.'

'Oui, I understand dog. Like the dead one we found in the lake' Retorted Paddy, keen to demonstrate his understanding of English.

'Of course' Said Ben 'The dead dog we found must have been Scarface's dog. That explains why it's not with him now. He must have been snooping around the reserve and his dog fell in the lake.'

'Poor thing' commiserated Lizzie 'I wonder how it happened?'

'I don't know' Said Ben 'but they seem to be checking the fence. What are they up to on a Sunday?'

As they watched him, the men could be seen to be looking closely at the fence wire and at the ground below. On one occasion Alan took out a tape measure and seemed to be measuring something. After 5 minutes he appeared to be satisfied. He then started pacing the distance from the electric security fence as far as the small trees growing nearby.

Apparently satisfied with his measurements Alan then stood upright, looking around him. When he turned towards Energy Heights the 3 children ducked out of sight.

'Do you think they saw us?' asked Lizzie, alarm showing on her face.

'I don't think so, but I can just about see where they were through this gap in the wooden planks' he replied.

For a second or two he tried to get into a suitable position to look through one of the gaps. Then he let out a call of alarm.

'They're coming over here' gasped Ben.

'They must have seen us' Whispered Lizzie

'I don't think so, but I'm not stopping to find out, come on' Said Ben, who immediately crawled towards the back of the hide and slipped out of the door, followed by his two pals. Keeping low they scuttled along the path away from the advancing men until they reached Electric Avenue, where they stopped to catch their breath.

'I'm going to have a peak with my binoculars from here' said Ben, and he carefully stood up behind the cover of a small willow tree. From where he was standing he was unable to see Alan, but he could clearly see the bird hide at Energy Heights. Then he saw a movement in the hide, followed by the familiar face of the New Deal man, at the window of the hide.

'They're in the hide' gasped Ben. If we'd stayed there they would have seen us. He gives me the creeps, does that Alan' Said Ben.

'What they do now?' Whispered a rather frightened looking Paddy.

'I can't see them now, they must have left.' Replied Ben.

'I hope they're not following us' Said Lizzie. 'Do you think we should move on a bit further?'.

'It's all right. I can see them now. They're walking back towards the Amphitheatre. I think they've finished now.' Whispered Ben. 'Let's go back to the hide'.

'You is certain?' Said Paddy, a worried look on his young face.

'Don't worry. He's going now. Look for yourself.' Encouraged Ben.

All three of them stood up behind the cover of the trees as the retreating figures made their way back along the fence line and eventually out of sight.

'Come on' Said Ben, unable to hide the excitement of the episode, from his voice. The three of them then returned to the hide.

'No sign of anything left behind' Said Lizzie. 'No reason why they should, I suppose. They were probably only looking around out of interest.' Then she noticed some numbers written in pencil on the windowsill of the hide.

'Look' she said 'this writing wasn't here before'

'What it say?' Enquired Paddy.

'2300 29 08' Replied Lizzie

'What does that mean? You can't be sure he wrote them though' Asked Ben.

'I was sitting just here before they came.' She replied. 'There is no way I would have missed them before. The numbers look a bit smeary. It looks like he must have spat on them and tried to wipe them off with his hand. Ergh, I'm not sitting there again' She said with a shiver.

The three children discussed the events and the numbers for some time.

'Could it be a telephone number?' suggested Ben.

They couldn't think what the numbers might mean and why Alan or Scarface might have been on the reserve on a Sunday.

'Are you going to tell your Dad?' asked Lizzie.

'I don't know. What is there for us to tell? One of his employees was taking a walk around the reserve on a pleasant Sunday morning. He thinks I'm daft enough already, especially if I tell him we ran away from him. Still I wonder what he was up to? I don't like him much. Let's just keep an eye open and think about what the numbers might mean.' Said Ben.

Chapter Eighteen
Dragonfly Goes Missing

The following Sunday, Ben decided to get up very early and go down to the reserve for a dawn chorus walk. He was well aware that most of the birds were well into their breeding season and were unlikely to be making too much noise. Getting up at 4am is never easy, but Ben was driven to try it just once during the summer holiday period to see what it was like.

As he walked through the streets a little later there were no signs of life, other than a few crows. He was a little nervous of them, having watched the famous Alfred Hitchcock film 'The Birds' only a few weeks earlier. But he decided that despite their coarse cawing sound, the crows were pretty well harmless. Nonetheless, as he walked he kept looking a little apprehensively over his shoulder to make sure the crows, or any other birds for that matter, were not following him.

As he entered the main gate of the reserve, the sun was just starting to rise, casting long shadows across the still dark waters of the lake. He suddenly felt much more relaxed about things, now he was in his own domain. The absence of human's on the reserve was nothing strange to him, with only the birds for company. A Cetti's warbler gave out a burst of sound from across the reserve, to be answered by a second one some distance to his left.

> 'Hey you down there!
> What you think you're doing?
> Why don't you go away?'

They seemed to shout at each other, a sound that forced a smile across his face.

He couldn't help saying out loud 'Alright, I know it's your territory! I'm just passing through.'

He decided to walk towards Troll's Bridge and then up past Butterfly Bank to the bird hide at Energy Heights. By the time he got to Troll's Bridge he was feeling wide awake and quite pleased to have ticked off a blackbird, reed warbler, jay, green woodpecker, dunnock, kingfisher and of course Cetti's warbler from his list of birds.

On reaching Troll's Bridge he rested against the handrail and looked over the side to see his own reflection in the narrow channel below. He took out one of the cereal bars his mum had thoughtfully put in his backpack the previous night

'Make sure you get some breakfast inside you. Young brains and bodies need feeding first thing in the morning' She had insisted.

She was of course right and Ben enjoyed the feeling of the chunks of cereal bar, as they slipped effortlessly down his throat and into his welcoming stomach. Dragonfly, the nature reserve's punt, was usually moored by Troll's bridge, where it was used as a platform for pulling the reeds that relentlessly encroached upon the narrow channel of water here.

As he stood leaning on the bridge handrail munching on the cereal bar, he realized that there was no sign of the punt. 'That's strange,' He said to himself 'It was there yesterday and there are still plenty of reeds to remove'.

Then his eye caught sight of the broken chain used to lock the punt in place. It had been cut through, leaving the remaining few links hanging from the bridge. Looking a little closer, Ben could see signs of heavy trampling of the bank-side vegetation and deep scarring marks in the surface of the path. The soil exposed by the scars looked very fresh, with the occasional boot print in the softer soil. It wasn't difficult for Ben to follow the marks that had been made, as the heavy punt was obviously dragged along the ground. It was then that Ben became aware that he was not the only human here, as voices called from the direction of Campion Path.

Someone had moved the punt fairly recently and he was pretty sure it was not the nature reserve's staff. Following the marks made in the path by the dragged punt, he moved cautiously in the direction of the river and towards the sound of raised voices.

When he got to Campion Path he realized that the voices were not coming from the reserve after all, but beyond the boundary fence, on the riverbank. If they had stolen the punt, how had they got it over the boundary fence he wondered? He quickly got his answer. The punt had evidently been dragged through the mass of brambles that grew here and through a massive hole cut in the fence using wire cutters.

He could still hear raised voices as someone struggled with the heavy boat at the edge of the river. He was now close enough to be able to see four men in the process of lowering the boat into the water of the river. Two of the men were standing at the bottom of the steep bank, close to the water, trying to ensure that the boat didn't capsize as it was slowly lowered down the bank. These two men were making a lot of noise, complaining about the weight and the fact that their feet were wet. Ben had seen neither man before.

However, at the top of the bank lowering the boat into the river were two figures he did recognize. One of them was hissing under his breath at his two noisier comrades 'Shut your racket, what's the point of stealing a boat at four in the morning, if you two wake up the whole neighbourhood with your shouting?'

It was the scar-faced gypsy he had spotted a few days earlier, talking to Alan. If seeing him was a surprise to Ben, the sight of the fourth member of the gang was even more alarming. It was Alan himself. Yet again apparently up to no good, although this time he had caught him red-handed.

Once the punt was in the water, three of them climbed in, whilst Alan remained on the bank holding the boat with the bow rope.

'OK, this is as far as I go' He said. 'If you want to nick the wheels off cars in the Suzuki compound, that's fine by me. You can borrow the punt, keep it, for all I care, but you're not getting me in it, on that river!'

And with that parting comment he threw the rope to the men in the punt, who quickly found themselves caught by the strong current and whipped away downstream. As the three men struggled to control the boat with the paddles it was evident that they were in for a challenging time. The boat spun around full-circle, before the two men with paddles managed to gain some sort of control as they disappeared downstream.

As they went, Alan turned and walked back towards where Ben was hiding in the undergrowth. Fortunately for Ben, instead of returning through the gap in the fence, where he would surely have discovered Ben, Alan continued walking briskly along the riverbank path, upstream towards Willow Close. Ben realized that he must be intent on putting some distance between him and the three villains in Dragonfly, judging by the pace he was setting.

Once Alan had gone, Ben breathed a sigh of relief. He was once again the only human on the nature reserve. What should he do now? The men had stolen Dragonfly and were about to use it to steal wheels from the four-wheel-drive cars parked in the Suzuki garage compound downstream.

It was actually a very clever and simple plan. He had noticed before that none of the warehouses and garages had CCTV cameras facing the nature reserve, but they fairly bristled with them facing the road. He also remembered how Old Danny had pointed out that the gypsies used the lake to hide their booty after breaking into the warehouses. The gang that had stolen Dragonfly must have been aware that there were no cameras at the Suzuki garage, other than those pointing towards the road. No one had considered that someone might break in from the riverside. The three waterborne villains were now about to make them pay for their mistake.

No one was likely to be about at four or five in the morning, but it was light enough by now for them to see what they were doing. They would probably moor beside the garage, cut through the fence, remove the expensive wheels off the cars, stack them in the punt and then float off downstream to the travelers' settlement, just below Bedford Bridge. Here they could unload the punt, hide the wheels and then let Dragonfly float downstream. Who would know how the wheels were stolen or where they might have gone?

For five more minutes Ben just sat where he was wondering what to do next. Finally he recalled the advice of the policeman in Felixstowe, the same advice he had followed when he reported Josh and his pals with their air-gun. Shaking a little, Ben dialed 999, half expecting no one to answer at 5am. To his surprise a voice appeared on the other end and asked him what service he wanted. Within a few minutes he had explained the situation and given his name and address.

When he had finished he sat for a minute or two thinking about what had happened. Dialing 999 had always seemed a bit scary to him. What would they say and would they tell him to stop wasting their time? Instead the operator had been very polite and even congratulated him on his good work. Ben felt a warm glow as he thought about how he had solved a crime. Well sort of. He considered creeping along the riverbank and watching the police arrive, but thought better of it. Instead he decided he had to share his adventure with someone. Lizzie and Paddy were the obvious ones, but they probably would not welcome him knocking on their doors at this unearthly hour.

So instead he decided to go home and tell his mum and dad. It was then that it dawned on him that he had not mentioned Alan's role to the police. He did however realize that he had to tell his dad about Alan. Dad would know what to do. So he set off back through the reserve, stopping to listen to the birds or watch for butterflies as he went. But his mind was no longer on the nature reserve; instead it was on the events he had just witnessed.

As he reached the road there were still no people around and no traffic, just the same cawing crows up on the lampposts, watching him moving below. Then the eerie silence was broken, by the sound of a car approaching from behind him. As he turned he saw that it was actually two police cars. Both cars carried non-uniformed passengers. On the back seat of the second car Ben got a fleeting glimpse of a face he recognized, with a butterfly shaped scar under his right eye. To his delight Ben realized they must have captured Scarface and his cronies.

Ben was almost shaking with excitement as he broke into a run, intent on telling his parents what had happened.

Chapter Nineteen
Ben's Reward

When he arrived home, Ben was jumping up and down with excitement, intent on telling his mum and dad what had happened, and about his part in it.

Much to his indignation, his parents were more than a little concerned when he told them about his discovery of the four men. It was just typical of parent's to worry about safety when the danger had already passed, especially when the adventure was surely the most important thing. His Dad was most concerned when Ben mentioned Alan's part in it all, particularly when he made mentioned of the clandestine meeting with Scarface, on the river bank a week or so earlier.

But by the end of the story, his parents could not hide their admiration and congratulated him for his initiative in calling the police. A little later a police officer called round and took a statement from Ben, who took great delight in telling the whole story over again.

His parents were so pleased with him that once the police officer had left, his dad offered him a reward.

'OK, young Sherlock Holmes, what kind of a treat do you think is worthy of a detective of your caliber?' Said his dad.

Ben thought for a while and then he knew exactly what he wanted. 'A night in the roundhouse' he said.

'Oh no!' Said Dad 'I'm not so sure about that'

'Oh please!' Pleaded Ben. 'You did say anything.' (which in actual fact they had not).

'Well I think he should be allowed to,' said Mum, much to both Ben and Dad's surprise.

'But you are the one who is always so concerned about his safety' replied Dad.

'Well I think he's old enough now.' Said his mum 'Ben has proved himself to be very responsible and we need to encourage that. Besides if we make sure he has his cell phone he can always call us on it. It's only a short drive to the reserve.

'OK. Young man, the roundhouse it is' said his dad and Ben jumped for joy with excitement.

It was now late enough to call round for Paddy and Lizzie. Off he went, hotfoot on his bike to share his news, leaving his rather bewildered parents to consider the wisdom of their agreement.

****

The next day was Monday. Although he was on his school holidays, Ben decided to go in to work with his Dad and do what he could to prepare the roundhouse for his sleep-over. As soon as he spotted Charlie he couldn't wait to tell him about the boat theft and share his good news with him about the roundhouse sleep-over. Charlie pulled his leg about creepy crawlies and ghosts that lived by the lake, in the usual way adults somehow feel the need to tease children, for no apparent reason. But Ben took it for what it was meant to be, just good-natured banter.

Then Dad called his usual Monday morning staff meeting and went through the key points of the forthcoming week's work.

'First of all you will have heard by now about the boat theft over the weekend.' Said Dad.

'Young Ben here has talked about nothing else since he came in' Said Charlie.

'Well thanks to him the police caught the villains red-handed. Dragonfly is a little damaged but not seriously. We can go and fetch her back from the river later and then repair the fence.' Said Dad.

'Hurray for Ben' Encouraged one of the reserve staff and they all clapped, much to Ben's embarrassment.

'Is it true about Alan?' Asked one of the team. 'I never liked him much and I'm not surprised that he was involved.'

'We have an eye-witness' Said Dad 'Ben saw him helping them steal the boat, although he wasn't involved in the wheel theft. I told the police, but they say they can't prosecute him, so it's up to us whether or not we bring charges. It's my intention to make it clear to Jackie at New Deal, that he is no longer welcome here and leave it at that.'

'Good riddance I say.' Added Charlie.

'Next item on the agenda. Things are looking pretty good for meeting Creamer's break-even demands. Thanks to Peter's work on the reserve and the financial contribution of the Environmental Trust, I think I can say in all confidence that we should meet the target set by Creamer and his mates. That means I'm confident that the reserve should stay open' Announced Dad.

The news brought smiles to everyone's faces and Ben was pleased to see his Dad smiling about his work for the first time in many weeks. It had obviously been weighing heavily on his shoulders, carrying the burden of ensuring none of the staff lost their jobs. He couldn't wait to tell Peter about it. He idolized Peter, a state of mind that was only added to by his contribution towards the reserves financial security.

'Where's Peter?' Asked Ben.

'He emailed me to say he won't be in for a few days.' Said his Dad. Then seeing Ben's disappointment he added 'But don't worry I'll email him back with the news and thank him as well.'

'OK' Said Ben, but he would have liked to have seen him nonetheless.

Right. I'd better ring Jackie and tell her about Alan.

****

'No? You're joking?' said Jackie when Dad broke the news to her about Alan. 'Oh that's terrible.'

'Of course it's out of the question for him to work here again.' Added Dad. He'd already decided not to mention Ben's part in it all, just to make sure there was no risk to him from Alan.

'Well he was due to come and see me first thing this morning, for a progress interview, but he's not shown up. I rang the number he gave me for contact purposes and got no answer. When I checked with Directory Enquiries they had no entry for him. Stranger still, the address he gave doesn't exist either, so I don't know how he's been getting his benefit payments? If he comes in though, I'll certainly tell him not to go down to you again. Bye now.' And she rang off.

As Dad put the phone down he noticed Ben standing by the door to his office.

'What is it?' Asked Ben, concerned by his dad's furrowed brow.

'Nothing important' Said Dad, 'It was Jackie, about Alan. Apparently he has disappeared. In fact it seems he never really existed, since he gave her a false telephone number and address.'

'Well as long as I don't have to see him again' Said Ben.

'Uh oh!' Said Dad, indicating towards the car park, 'It's Creamer again'

Ben looked in the direction of the car park and saw the distinctive shape of Dad's boss striding purposefully towards the nature reserve offices.

As he watched, Ben saw him pause briefly to talk to Charlie. They exchanged a few brief sentences; with Creamer looking a bit agitated by whatever Charlie was telling him. Then he strode purposefully and grim-faced towards his dad's office.

'What's all this rubbish about a boat theft?' Said Creamer, without even a "good-day" first. He didn't even acknowledge Ben's presence in the room.

Dad had a weary look on his face as he answered. 'It's true. Three men were caught red-handed loading stolen wheels into the reserve's punt. They stole it, cut the fence, dragged it down to the river and then floated it down to the Suzuki dealers.'

'But what's this rubbish about Alan being involved? Did the police arrest him as well?' Questioned Creamer.

'No they didn't, but he did help them steal the punt, before they took it down the river.' Said Dad.

'How do they know he helped them steal it, if the police didn't catch him?' pressed Creamer.

'There was a witness. Ben watched the whole thing.' Said Dad.

'A boy! You're taking the word of a boy?' Said Creamer, raising his voice as he spoke.

'No.' Said Dad 'Not a boy, but Ben. My son. The one that's standing behind you. The one you chose not to notice when you came in'

Dad was on his feet by this time, a look on his face, which hid none of his irritation with Creamer. But if Creamer noticed his irritation, he didn't show it.

'What does Alan have to say about it? Where is he?' Asked Creamer.

'Alan has not come in today. And if he does he'll be told to turn round and go straight back home. I've already rung New Deal to tell them to place him somewhere else on the scheme.' Said Dad.

'What!' Creamer erupted. 'You sacked him? You sacked him on the word of a boy? And you didn't even get Alan's version of the story? Well I'm afraid that's not good enough. You just ring them back and tell them you've changed your mind!'

By this time Dad had reached boiling point. Ever since he had met Creamer he had been swallowing the words he longed to use to tell him how he felt. His remarks about Ben and his bullying tone were just too much. The floodgates opened.

'Listen you.' He said, pointing his finger at Creamer. 'When Ben tells me he saw Alan stealing the punt, I don't need any more proof. Alan is trouble. What's more he gave Jackie a false address and telephone number. We probably won't see him again anyway, because he's probably half way to Glasgow by now!'

Creamer just stared at Dad before collecting himself enough to say. 'Don't you talk to me like that, otherwise you'll find yourself out of a job'

'Quite frankly Mr. Creamer, I don't care about you or the job. We've met your budget target and deadline. So there's no reason for the reserve to be closed. I suggest you leave now before I get really cross. You wouldn't like that!' Dad spat the words out through gritted teeth.

Ben just stared at Dad. Creamer stared at Dad. Who wouldn't? He was a terrifying sight to behold. Ben wasn't sure how much he liked his dad losing his temper, but it was an awesome experience. Creamer was anything but in awe. He just turned round and walked out of the office, all colour drained from his face. Looking straight ahead he walked past Charlie without a word, got into his car and drove down the drive.

'And good riddance to you!' Dad whispered after Creamer. 'But I don't expect we've heard the last from him.'

'Wow Dad, you were tremendous' Said Ben, all agog.

'I'm afraid I rather lost control. Probably not my finest hour, but enough's enough.

'Can I help Dad?' Asked Ben.

'No, thanks Ben. I've got some paperwork to do. Why don't you ask Charlie to check the roundhouse out for you in preparation for tonight?'

'Great' Said Ben and scuttled out of the door to find Charlie.

****

As Ben approached the roundhouse that evening he felt like some kind of Midwest pioneer. He could have been miles away from the rest of the world, instead of within a mile of several thousand other human souls. On reaching the roundhouse he laid out his sleeping bag and sorted through his supplies.

Once all was sorted out he climbed into the sleeping bag and plugged in his mp3 player. The sun was setting rapidly as the light started to fade. However he wasn't sleepy yet, so he decided to climb out of the bag and explore in the half-light. Snake Island lay just across the lake and he thought it would be fun to make his way to the tip of the island as an adventure in the dark. Despite the best efforts of the reserve staff, no otters had as yet visited the artificial holt built at the end of the island. The access to the island was across a narrow wooden plank, which could be withdrawn to discourage foxes and humans from getting onto the island and disturbing nesting birds.

Ben carefully placed the plank across the narrow channel that separated the island and the mainland. In the half-light he had some trouble getting the plank in place. Eventually he managed to fix both ends in place and began crossing. In his haste he had failed to see that the far end of the plank was not fixed very securely. Halfway across he felt the plank twisting slightly to his left. He compensated by leaning to his right.

Suddenly his foot slipped and within the blink of an eye he was up to his knees in mud and water. Realizing what had happened, he at first let out an oath, followed by a burst of laughter at his predicament. Eventually he was able to haul himself back onto the plank and inch his way along it on his belly. A little undignified but effective. There came a plopping sound and he froze for a second, wondering if one of the lake's pike might be out hunting. This thought caused the hairs on the back of his neck to rise and he scuttled double quick along the plank.

Once on the other side he located the end of the plank a little more securely and using the torch from his pocket he inspected the damage. Dirty wet trainers, jeans soggy up to his knees and little else. Oh well he thought that's what adventures are for.

Slipping and scrambling along in the dark he made his way along the narrow dirt path towards the tip of Snake Island. Eventually, after much slipping and sliding, he somehow found his way to the tip of the island and sat next to the artificial otter holt. This was a collection of logs and covering branches placed here in the hope of attracting otters. He was now looking directly across at Kingfisher Hide. After 5 minutes staring into the blackness he realized that adventures alone can be a bit boring, unless you are doing something. Sitting alone in the dark was not his idea of excitement, so he decided to make the return trip along the island and back over the plank. This time he was more careful and achieved the crossing without any problems. However, he decided to leave the plank where it was, rather than risk moving it in the dark.

    Much more tired than he had been when he began his adventure, he finally found his way back to the roundhouse, where he slipped off his wet shoes, socks and jeans and climbed into his sleeping bag. Excitement quickly gave way to exhaustion and he dropped off into a deep, undisturbed sleep.

    As he slept various scuttlings in the undergrowth went un-noticed, insects and spiders wandered freely about on the floor of the roundhouse, pausing briefly to inspect this new warm mass that occupied their territory, before getting on with their daily round of chores. Oblivious to these nocturnal comings and goings Ben disappeared into dreamland.

Chapter Twenty
Plotters at Hornbeam Horseshoe

Nothing disturbed Ben until the early hours of the morning. As he awoke he briefly wondered where he was. Then he recalled that he was sleeping in the roundhouse. He wondered why he had woken up and checked his watch. It was 3am. Perhaps a bird or some other creature had made a noise? Still tired, he turned over and decided to go back to sleep.

Then he heard murmuring. It sounded like human voices coming towards where he lay in the roundhouse. Who could be moving about the woods at this ungodly hour he wondered? Perhaps one of the fishermen like old Danny, some of whom unfortunately left their rubbish behind on the river bank. Normally they climbed through the fence by the Sluice Gate rather than bothering coming up here, where the fishing was poor and the fence too difficult to climb. He decided to inch his way towards the door and peer out into the night.

As he struggled to see anything he tensed a little, listening again. The voices were coming closer. He fumbled for his cell phone wondering if he should call his parents. But it wasn't in his pocket. Where could it be? Then he realized what had happened. The plopping sound he had heard when he crossed over the plank to Snake Island was not a fish, but his cell phone slipping out of the pocket of his jeans.

Now he was all-alone, in the dark, with strange voices coming towards him at three in the morning. He just froze and listened.

Most of the voices were loud enough for him to hear what was being said, in the still of the night, although he did have trouble picking up every detail. Their owners had stopped at what he realized was the clearing called Hornbeam Horseshoe and were sitting on the log circle discussing something not 30 metres from where he lay.

As he strained his ears he was able to pick up most of what they said.

'Ok, let's stop here for a few minutes and talk through the plan' said a woman's voice. It was not a local accent, but sounded more like the voice of someone well bred. It was a voice he was sure he had heard somewhere before.

'Do we have to?' said a quietly spoken man's voice. He sounded fairly young and well spoken also and was obviously not best pleased with life in the dark woods. 'I hate places like this, especially in the dark. Give me a medical laboratory any day, at least the animals are not likely to crawl up your trouser leg there'

'Stop bleating.' Came a third voice. 'I'd rather be in the dark of the woods than standing in the open with a police searchlight trained on me'. This voice sounded distinctly different from the other's, Irish perhaps.

'Yeah.' Came yet another familiar voice. 'I rather like it here. It's not as spooky as the humming noise coming from the electricity compound.'

Whose voice was that? Ben struggled to put a face to it.

'Hey, there's the roundhouse over there. Why don't we sit down in there?' The familiar voice came again.

Ben froze at the prospect of them discovering him and what they might do.

'No this will do just fine. We're not on a Sunday-school holiday you know. Just sit down so we can discuss plans.' Commanded the woman's voice. Ben breathed a sigh of relief.

The moon was up now and as the few clouds in the sky cleared, the light of the moon enabled him to see the four figures gathered in a huddle, as he lay in the roundhouse as stiff as a board, now too terrified to move.

The woman's voice was commanding and made Ben realize that she was the ringleader. She certainly was not one of the local fishermen.

'OK, so you've seen the electricity compound. What's the best way of getting in there, laying a charge next to the transformers and then getting out? That electrified fence looks pretty effective'

'Shouldn't be a problem getting in. 'Came the familiar male voice again. 'We just use picks to dig our way under the wire. I can't understand why The Grid don't put concrete footings in. All we've got to do is dig out the pebbles and wriggle under. Piece-er-cake. Then it's up to Sean here to lay the charges and Bob's yer uncle'

'How do you know that it will be as easy as all that' came the voice of the Irishman, Sean. 'Do you work for the Grid or are yi just guessin' perhaps?'

'You don't have to work for them to know their weaknesses and as you know I have been working at the nature reserve for a week or two now. Long enough to case the substation and to make a few useful local contacts. I've been doing some talking to one of the guys from the travelers' camp over the way. He and his mates have broken into half a dozen of the Grid's substations in recent years. All they do is dig a trench under the security fences, nick the copper earthing straps from the electrical plant inside, get back out through the trench and backfill the holes before dawn. Dead easy. No-one is even aware that the stuff has been nicked, because they cover all traces of their activity.'

It was then that Ben realized who the speaker was, Alan the New Deal placement. Yet again he'd come across the man on the nature reserve at strange times of the day. Now he understood why he and Scarface had been checking the substation boundary fence the other Sunday morning. He was finding out how to break in.

'Why didn't you bring him with you tonight?' Questioned the young educated voice. 'I'd like to have heard it all from the horses mouth'

'Sorry, he said he couldn't make it tonight. He had some other business to attend to. But he explained the whole setup to me. No problems there.'

'What does he know about our operation?' Asked Sean. 'I don't like too many people knowing our business.'

'Don't worry' Reassured Alan. 'He thinks I'm just interested in petty theft. In fact I fixed him up with a few stolen items, just as a goodwill gesture. He's happy enough now'

'Happy indeed!' Thought Ben. 'Taking a few weeks holiday in a police cell more likely.' Now Ben understood the deal with the black plastic sack and why they were casing the substation fence together. It was all falling into place. These four were just a bunch of burglars looking to steal copper from the substation. Or that was what Ben assumed they were up to.

'OK' said the woman, 'then it's over to you Sean, or whatever your real name is'.

'As far as you are concerned my name is Sean. Don't you be worryin' about me darlin' ' He replied with the confidence of a man who has been in similar situations before. 'I can blow anything from a padlock to a nuclear power station. As long as we can be away from here long before it blows then I'll be well pleased.'

'You might be far away, but some of us will be busy up at the science park liberating those poor unfortunate monkeys and beagles, whilst you're back on the plane to Belfast and the comforts of home.' Grumbled the younger man with the more educated voice.

'Listen' replied Sean, 'my part in all this is to blow up your transformers, nothing more. Personally I don't give a dam about your four-legged friends or your animal liberation crap. You contacted our organization to provide the explosives know-how and that's what you're getting'

'And a nice big wedge of money you're getting for it too' added the younger man.

'OK' interrupted the woman, 'you do your job Sean and we'll do what we have to do, but do you foresee any problems?'

'None at all' replied Sean 'As long as smarty-pants here can provide me with all the ingredients I need'

'Don't worry. You'll have all you need within a couple of days'

'Well I'm so glad to here it' continued the Irishman, 'You may not know this, but some years ago the substation was on the IRA's hit-list. They wanted to knock it out as part of the mainland terror campaign. It looks like I might get to blow it after all. Should make a nice big bang and cause a lot of people a big headache trying to replace the power to most of East Kent'

'With most of East Kent losing its power, we should have no problem breaching the lab's security system and releasing the animals' chipped in Alan.

'Fine then,' the woman continued 'Sean gets paid off, courtesy of my father, and we get to draw people's attention to the use of animals for cosmetic and medical testing.' Ben struggled to place her voice. He was certain he knew it.

'OK, when do we do the job?' She asked the group.

'Personally I prefer a full moon.' Answered Alan. 'I don't want to be tripping over things in the dark, what about you Sean?'

'No. Same for me. A bit of moon-light is no problem. Like in the old Irish song "By the Rising of the Moon". A good traditional time for a bit of Irish action. I suppose you might call it a Bomber's Moon.' Sean said with an ironic grin. 'I'm happy with the date agreed earlier. That suit you, Miss Money-bags?'

Ben had been listening carefully to most of what they had said. As the conversation unfolded he grew more and more alarmed that these were not the kind of people he wanted to catch him snooping. The Irishman called Sean was furthest away, with a soft Irish accent that Ben found hard to hear properly. He had picked up that they were considering doing something to the substation. Perhaps they were burglars, perhaps not? He could certainly imagine the shifty looking Alan being a burglar, but not the younger man, or the well-spoken woman. And what about the Irishman? What was he doing in Kent? It was a long way to come to burgle a substation. What could a substation have that was of value to burglars? And what was it they had said about a Bomber's Moon? Whatever that was!

Nonetheless, he was certain that he didn't want to stay in the Roundhouse a moment longer. Very carefully he slipped out of his sleeping bag to get as far away from the interlopers as he could. He was able to slip out of the doorway and round the back of the roundhouse, heading in the direction of the riverbank and safety.

As he checked over his shoulder to make sure no-one had spotted him, he failed to notice the young bramble vine that was strung across the path, hidden by the shadows. Suddenly he was tumbling headlong into a patch of nettles. He suppressed a shout as he felt the nettle leaves sting his face.

Brave as it was of him to stifle his cry of pain, the noise of his fall attracted unwanted attention from elsewhere in the woods.

'What was that noise?' shouted the man with the educated voice. 'Could it be someone listening in on us perhaps?'

'Calm down college boy,' said Alan, 'who's going to be out in the in the woods at this time of night? The substation security company never does more than cruise up and down the substation slip-road in their dog van and they certainly don't come wandering out through the woods at three in the morning. It's most likely a young fox on the prowl'

'So you might say, know all, but I'm going to check anyway.' And he got up and headed in the direction of the now prostrate and severely stung Ben.

The man was busy checking the undergrowth with a long stick and sweeping the area with his torch. As he got closer Ben wondered what to do. Should he stay still and hope the man wouldn't see him? Or was he better off making a run for it. Both options were fraught with risks.

The man was getting closer. Within a second or two he would discover Ben, and then what?

His mind made up, he was just about to make a dash for it in his bare feet and underpants, when an almighty kafuffle erupted from the bushes about two or three metres away to his left. The man wielding the long stick had spooked a roosting cock pheasant.

As the bird burst from the cover of the woods, it let out a night splitting cry as its wings flapped powerfully. The young man jumped back in shock at the noise and the sight of a large bird flapping wildly to escape from the threat that had spooked it. Next second the large bird collided with the young man's head, causing him to overbalance and fall head-long into the nettles not two metres from the prostrate and very uncomfortable figure of Ben.

As the bird flew off terrified into the night sky, the woman ran over to help her fallen comrade. He could hear Alan hooting loudly from Hornbeam Horseshoe, laughing at the hapless animal activist.

'I suppose we'd better run before the pheasant has the law on us?' he cackled.

'Oh shut your face' was all the reply he got.

'Where are my glasses?' He said to himself, obviously flustered by the whole episode.

'They are probably in amongst the undergrowth' said his female companion, turning her torch back in Ben's direction and scanning the ground.

As the two of them searched the undergrowth for the fallen spectacles, the full moon appeared momentarily from behind a cloud and Ben got a good clear look at both of their faces.

The man was the guy who had been lurking around the substation taking photographs on the day of the cross country race, whilst the woman was none other than Erica Butler, the leader of the adult group his dad had been showing around the reserve just a few weeks earlier.

The two of them were no more than a metre or two from where Ben lay rigid with fear. They might discover him at any moment and then what?

Then the woman paused, not more than a metre from Ben.

'Here they are Ian.' She said as she bent down to pick them up, within touching distance of Ben. 'Be more careful, we don't want anyone to hear us you know?'

As the two of them turned away from Ben she shouted in her commanding voice to the rest of the group. 'Come on it's time we went back to the car. We can discuss the details elsewhere.'

'You look like you might need some calamine lotion on those stings' She said not particularly sympathetically to her comrade. 'You'll look a right mess at the university in the morning'.

And with that the four of them turned and headed towards the hole in the fence near Willow Close, where Ben assumed their car was parked.

He could now put faces and names to three of the four plotters. It sounded as though they were going to do something to the substation, but he couldn't think what and he wasn't sure when, other than the mention of the 'Bomber's Moon'.

Once they were well away Ben picked himself out of the nettle patch and returned to the Roundhouse to inspect the damage to his badly nettled arms and legs. Fortunately for him his mother had supplied him with sting relief cream, which he applied thickly over the nettled areas. Rather than risk coming across the interlopers again he decided to stay put and crawled back into his sleeping bag, thinking about what to tell his parents. If he told them everything they'd surely never let him stay out in the woods again, but he felt he had to tell someone about what he had heard.

Within a few minutes the stinging was starting to subside sufficiently for him to fall asleep, mentally and physically exhausted by all that had happened that night. As he drifted off into unconsciousness he resolved to talk to Lizzie and Paddy, about what he should do.

Chapter Twenty One
A Chance to Ponder

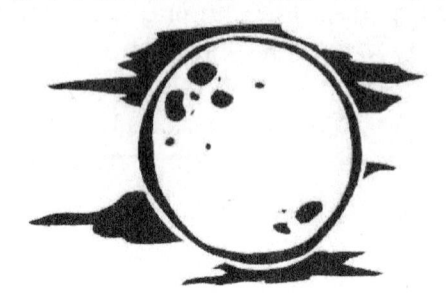

As the early morning sun broke through the tall tree canopy of Canterbury Woods, the gloom of the Roundhouse slowly withdrew. Ben lay fast asleep whilst the woodland around him awoke to another day.

Meanwhile Ben was encountering the kind of experience that thankfully only occurs in dreams. He was dreaming he was in the hutch of his pet rabbit Frizzbie. Strangely, the hutch was round in shape, with a thatched roof and a small campfire smouldering in the middle of it. He was able to see through the chicken wire across the front of the hutch into the yard at the back of his house. It all looked very familiar, but much bigger than normal. From out of the dark, beyond the garden wall there came a scrabbling noise, as though someone were climbing it. Suddenly the shape of a hooded figure appeared over the wall, followed by three others.

'Here's the hutch,' Said the smallest of the figures, a woman. 'Dam they've locked it!'

'Stand back.' Commanded the voice of one of the others, in a thick Irish accent. 'I'll have to dynamite it'

Terror gripped Ben. He ran to the back of the hutch, where Frizzbie was already cowering amongst the straw. Suddenly there came a deafening noise and then he felt hands gather him up roughly and throw him into a smelly sack.

'Let's get out of here.' Came the woman's commanding voice. Ben felt the sack, with him inside, being thrown over someone's shoulder as they made their getaway. It felt as though he was being carried for a long time, thrown from side to side inside the sack, as the person carrying him ran.

Suddenly the running stopped and he heard voices again. The sack was swung again, downwards this time and he felt himself being laid gently on the ground.

'Out you come little fella.' Came a man's voice. 'We won't harm you, you're safe now'. The end of the sack opened and hands lifted him up and placed him on the ground. As he looked around him he could see he was in the middle of Hornbeam Horseshoe. Everything looked so big and strange. Next to him he could see Frizzbie hopping around sniffing at the ground.

'Got to go now.' Came one of the voices. 'More animals to rescue tonight'. And off they dashed.

All became silent except for the sound of the wind in the tree canopy. Then Ben noticed Frizzbie sit up on his hind legs and sniff the air. His ears twitched slightly and

Ben realized what it was that he had heard. There was a rustling sound coming from the area of nettles to his right.

Frizzbie suddenly scuttled into the darkness on the other side of the clearing, obviously frightened by whatever it was that had made the sound. The sound seemed to be getting louder. Something big was moving through the undergrowth in his direction.

Ben just froze with fear. Then a large head appeared, covered in sleek brown hairs that continued along the length of its long powerful, shiny wet body. It looked like a large stoat or weasel. Ben realized it was a mink, probably one that had escaped from a mink farm, released by his dark liberators on some previous raid. Gripped by fear Ben immediately tried to run. He felt his legs pumping hard to get away from the enormous creature that stood before him, but it was no good. He just couldn't move.

It was then that the mink charged at him, its sharp, bared, white teeth glistening in the moonlight. As he felt the creature's jaws close around him, Ben felt angry. Why couldn't they have left him in his hutch? He was happy and safe there. He really didn't want to be a wild animal at all.

****

Ben awoke with a start. His forehead felt sweaty and something sharp was digging into his left wrist. When he looked down he was surprised to see the fingers of his right hand digging nails into his skin. Then he remembered the dream and realized where he was.

'Hell. So that's what it must be like to be a wild creature' He muttered. Then he remembered the events of the night before and realized that he had to do something to stop the plotters getting away with their planned raid on the substation and animal laboratories.

What should he do? If he told his parents what had happened, they'd probably never let him come to the Roundhouse again. He decided to talk to Lizzie and Paddy. After all a problem shared is a problem halved, as he recalled being told many times.

It was 7am. Sunday morning. Most kids of his age would not be crawling out of bed for another 3 or 4 hours, but then few of them had spent the night in a house made of logs, reeds and mud, in the middle of a wood. He packed all his gear and made his way home, ready for the cooked breakfast his mum said she'd cook him if he promised not to get eaten by wild animals. That was her joke, but probably partly explained his nightmare.

'Thanks Mum.' He said to himself.

When he got home Mum was already up. Despite the early hour she was pretty chirpy, happy to see him back home, safe and sound.

She rustled up some bacon and eggs for him, asking him questions about the night before. Ben just grunted words like 'OK' and 'Fine' whenever she tried to get information from him. Realizing that she was wasting her time she decided to return to bed, with the Sunday papers for a long read.

'At least I might get some information out of these!' She smiled, as she ruffled his uncombed hair on her way out of the kitchen door.

Ben knew that Lizzie would be up by now, as she went horse riding at 9am, but would be busy mucking-out the stables by 8am. He decided to walk down to the stables and tell her about last night's events.

When he arrived at the stables one of the loosebox doors was wide open. Ben guessed Lizzie must be inside. As he approached he could hear the unmistakable sound of Lizzie being busy, humming a nameless tune as she scooped up the horse leftovers into a wheelbarrow.

'Hi Lizzie' He said.

'Hello Ben, what brings you out of your bed at this hour on a Sunday morning? Need some exercise mucking out horses? You'll find a fork over there.' smiled Lizzie, indicating towards the corner.

'Well not really' he said 'I really wanted to ask your advice about something.'

'Sounds a bit heavy' Answered Lizzie. 'OK, I'll be your agony aunt, but only if you lend me a hand'

'If I must,' replied Ben with little enthusiasm, as he reluctantly sauntered over to the corner and picked up the fork.

'I spent last night in the Roundhouse' Began Ben.

'Wow, great fun' Said Lizzie standing up and showing more interest in what Ben had to say. 'Bit scary was it? Did you stay all night or did you scurry home at the first owl's hoot?' She laughed.

'Well actually it was a bit scary' said Ben and he continued to relate the whole night's activities to Lizzie.

Lizzie stopped what she was doing when he got to the bit about the voices at Hornbeam Horseshoe. All she could say was 'No?' as the tale unfolded, with Ben going into detail about what happened and what he thought he had heard.

By the time he had finished Lizzie had stopped working completely. She just stared open mouthed at him.

'Is this for real?' She said.

'Of course it is!' Said Ben, showing some hurt. 'Do you think I could make up a story like that?'

'Of course not' Soothed Lizzie. 'What are you going to do? Are you going to tell your Dad?'

'What do I tell him? Do you think he'd believe me? The most likely thing is that he and Mum would ban me from going to the woods alone again. I'm not taking that risk.' Said Ben emphatically.

'OK' Soothed Lizzie, 'But let's just examine everything that you know. There are four people plotting to do something to the substation, but you don't know what. You overheard them in the woods. You think you can identify three of them. You don't know when they are going to do this thing or how?

'Not much to tell anyone really, even if I knew who to tell.' Admitted Ben.

'Perhaps we should do nothing for the moment. Alan no longer works at the nature reserve and the other two you think you could identify don't have anything to do with the nature reserve. The whole electricity compound is surrounded by high voltage electric fencing. The place has regular security patrols, according to the signs all around it. So what are the chances of anyone doing anything? Perhaps you didn't hear everything clearly. After all you were some distance away from them when they were talking and you had only just woken up in the middle of the night.' Reasoned Lizzie.

Ben was feeling less sure of himself now.

'Do you want me to talk to my Dad about it?' She offered.

'No. He'll only tell my Dad and then they'll probably stop me going to the Roundhouse overnight again.' Said Ben. 'Let's just leave it for a while and think about it.'

Ben left Lizzie shoveling horse manure and straw and made his way back home, thinking to himself about the previous night's events and what he should do. He was feeling distinctly unsure of himself now and really didn't want to talk to his parents about it. For the moment he thought he'd best keep quiet, rather than make a fool of himself.

****

As August was drawing to a close, Ben was starting to think about the coming school year and wishing the summer would just last forever.

He'd had some great times with Paddy and Lizzie, exploring the nature reserve and occasionally further a-field. They had taken their bikes one day and cycled up to The Blean, the ancient woodlands on the hill overlooking Canterbury. The hill was so steep that they had really walked most of it, pushing their bikes, with the hot August sun making Ben wish that he could just dump it at the side of the road. Of course their reward was the high-speed return journey back down through the university grounds.

Paddy would be returning to Nice in a few days time. He had made good friends with Paddy and was sad that they would soon be separated by the whole of France. Paddy's mum had got on well with Ben's mum and dad. As a last goodbye they had invited Paddy's mum and his sister Valentine to a barn dance being run by the local wildlife trust. Lizzie's parents would also be going.

The three youngsters agreed to baby-sit Ben's younger sister Beth whilst their parents were out. Once they had got Beth off to bed, they settled down to watch a film. Ben had been able to hire a DVD of the Matrix. To Paddy's delight they played it with the French subtitles turned on.

Over the last week or so Ben had been happier because of the more relaxed atmosphere at home now that Dad was confident of meeting Creamer's deadline. Despite the bust-up with Creamer, Dad was of the opinion that his boss would just have to live with it.

At the back of Ben's mind though doubts nagged about the four people he had overheard plotting at Hornbeam Horseshoe. He wanted to warn his Dad, but didn't feel confident about what it all meant. What's more, he didn't want to do anything that might spoil the much-improved atmosphere at home. However, he had resolved that he would have to tell Dad in the morning, but not before his parent's had enjoyed their night out together.

All he knew about the plotters was that they were a threat to the substation, but he was uncertain as to how, or when. All he had to go on were the numbers left by Alan and Scarface and something about a 'Bomber's Moon'.

As the credits ran at the end of the film, Paddy and Ben decided to be Neo and Agent Smith fighting it out to the death.

Lizzie watched them with some amusement. 'What shall we do now?' Said Lizzie. 'It's ten thirty. The grown-ups won't be back until midnight.'

'I know.' Said Ben. 'Let's look at Teletext and find out what's on.'

He pressed the Teletext button on the remote controller and the Teletext screen sprang out from the TV. As it did Ben just stared at the screen, his mouth open, his thoughts racing.

'What is it?' Asked Paddy seeing the look on Ben's face.

'Bomber's Moon' Said Ben

'What that?' Said Paddy

'Bomber's Moon.' Ben repeated more loudly. 'Bomber's Moon.'

'What?' Said Lizzie a bit bewildered by Ben's attitude.

'Look!' Said Ben pointing at the Teletext screen.

As they all looked at the screen Ben read out the headline. 'Bomber's Moon Tonight'

'So what does it mean?' Asked Lizzie, not really understanding what Ben was getting at.

'Bomber's Moon, that's what the gang said at Hornbeam Horseshoe.' Explained Ben and he clicked the controller to reveal the rest of the story.

'Over much of England, tonight's moon is likely to be the brightest for many years. With the exception of Southern England, where strong winds and rain are forecast, the clear skies and the full moon over the rest of the country will provide the best Bomber's Moon since World War Two.' Read Ben.

'Bomber's Moon, Full Moon. It's tonight. They are going to attack the substation tonight.

'Tonight?' Questioned Lizzie. 'Is that all you've got to go on?'

'They said they were going to carry out their raid at the next Bomber's Moon. That's tonight!'

'When they attack?' Asked Paddy.

'I don't know' Said Ben.

'No, but I do!' Exclaimed Lizzie.

'How?' Said Paddy

'The numbers. Do you remember the numbers 29 08 23 00? The one's Alan wrote down at Energy Heights? Well just look at the top right hand corner of the screen.'

As they looked at the screen Ben read the date out loud '29 Aug 22:30.'

Then he understood what Lizzie meant. '29 08 is today's date, the 29th of August.' Said Ben.

'And 22.30 is the time. Said Lizzie.

In half an hour it will be 23.00.' Said Ben. 'That's when they'll attack!'

Chapter Twenty Two
The Stake-out

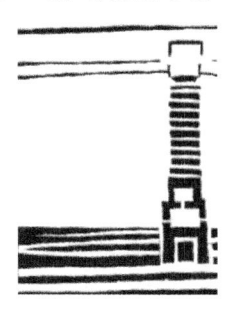

'What we do?' Said Paddy, once he realized what Lizzie and Ben were talking about.

'What did they say they were going to do?' Asked Lizzie, in her usual way of taking control.

'Break in to the substation, I think.' Said Ben a little defensively. 'Perhaps they are going to steal something?'

'We tell Lizzie's father n'est pas?' said Paddy.

'But he's at the Barn Dance with everyone else,' said Ben, now becoming agitated by the delay, 'and there's not enough time.'

'We could dial 999.' suggested Lizzie.

'And tell them what?' Asked Ben. 'The police wouldn't believe us. No, I'm going to go down there and check it out first. If I see something then I'll get the police.'

'You can't go on your own' Said Lizzie 'and I'm supposed to be baby-sitting Beth. What happens if she wakes up?'

'I come' Said Paddy.

'OK' Said Ben. 'You stay here Lizzie and we'll call you if there is any problem'

'I don't like it' Worried Lizzie. 'It might be dangerous'

'Don't worry, we'll be very careful' said Ben reassuringly.

With that Ben and Paddy put on their coats and boots and headed off down to the nature reserve. Outside, the forecast rain was already coming down quite heavily, with a gusty wind blowing it into their faces as they approached the main gate to the reserve and the substation.

Despite the rising moon on the eastern horizon, it was very dark on the reserve. The rain was still coming down heavily, made worse by the rising wind, as the weather front rolled in from the west. There would be no bomber's moon here tonight thought Ben. The reserve was not at its most hospitable tonight. Shaking with a mix of fear and excitement they made their way along The Fox Road and World Record Walk, thankful of the cover provided by the dark.

The pylon bird towered above them as they picked their crouching way behind any tall grass or bushes that afforded suitable cover. Peter had finally finished the bird, adding its head and threatening beak. The massive sculpture looked well capable of attacking anyone who came within pecking distance of it. Ben paused for a second and catching Paddy's attention, silently indicated a hole cut in the outer fence of the reserve. It was obviously a new cut, with the long grass adjacent to the hole flattened by the recent passing of feet. This was obviously the route taken by the gang, doubtless heading for the point that Alan and Scarface had chosen to break into the compound.

Picking their way through the trees of Broad Oak Woods they avoided getting too close to the compound, preferring to circle round and come out at a point mid-way between The Amphitheatre and Energy Heights.

'Stay close to the trees' said Ben,

'OK' Said Paddy, following Ben as he moved, still in a crouched position, towards the compound fence just below Energy Heights. Despite the dark they were close enough to the compound to make out the shapes of the transformers that Ben recalled the plotters were intending to attack. They both froze in the cover of some small trees, peering into the gloom for any signs of life inside.

'Ecouter' Said Paddy, holding his right hand to his ear and pointing with his left hand towards Energy Heights. 'I hear voices'.

Sure enough as Ben listened, he too could hear a whispered discussion coming from the bird hide.

'They are here' Said Ben 'Time to call the police I think'

Ben was pleased that he had remembered to bring his cell phone. As he took it out of his pocket he quickly dialed the local police number, but nothing happened.

'No signal' Said Paddy, pointing to the left side of Ben's cell-phone. 'Why not?'

'Must be the electric substation killing the signal' Said Ben. 'Damn, I didn't think about that.'

'What we do now?' Asked Paddy

'Do you think you could find your way to Peter's house, his place is nearer than mine?' Asked Ben.

Paddy nodded his head.

'Tell Peter what is happening and get him to ring the police.' Instructed Ben.

'Yes I go,' said Paddy, a serious look on his face. 'What you do?'

'I'll stay here and watch what happens.' Said Ben reassuringly.

'OK.' Whispered Paddy.

'Go now.' Said Ben.

Paddy gave Ben a reassuring smile and then disappeared into the rain, back along the route they had just come. Ben felt very alone. Not for the first time he was on the nature reserve, in the dark, with some suspicious characters plotting who-knows-what nearby.

Once again he squatted down, watching the driving rain causing the electrical apparatus in the compound to buzz loudly. He could see little where he crouched, but was able to hear the distant hum of conversation coming from Energy Heights. As always, curiosity got the better of him and he resolved to creep a little closer to the bird hide and try to listen to the discussions of the gang up there.

Five minutes of careful climbing up the slope brought him to the front of the bird hide. From within he could hear familiar voices.

'Doesn't look like the weather's going to break.' Came the voice of the woman Erica.

'No matter.' Replied the Irish brogue of Sean. 'The Irish are used to a bit of rain you know? You coming?'

'Lead on McDuff or whatever your name is' Came the familiar voice of Alan. 'Got mi spade. Probably only take us five minutes to dig under the wire, into the compound and then it's all up to you.'

With that the two men could be heard opening the door to the bird hide, which squeaked through lack of oil. Then they were gone, leaving just Erica and Ian behind.

'Shall we leave those two to it then?' Said the man's voice.

'I believe they are quite capable of managing on their

own.' Replied Erica. 'We need to be making our way up to the laboratories and organize things up there. Once the substation transformers have been knocked out, we'll need to move fairly quickly to break into the primate section and get the monkeys out, before anyone connects the black-out with any potential break-in up there.'

It was only then that Ben realized what was going on. 'Hell!' He thought to himself. 'I hope Paddy gets Peter and the police soon, otherwise this is going to be a bit messy.'

'Before we go let's just go over the details one more time.' Said Erica in the commanding tones that fitted perfectly with her stern face and no-nonsense manner.

Ben decided it was time to move to where he could get a better view of Alan and the Irishman. Very quietly he crept away from the bird hide, down the steps at Rock Down, along the path by Newt Pond Scruffits and back through Broad Oak Woods as far as The Valley of Death. From here he was able to pick his way up through the trees to a vantage position overlooking where he thought Alan and Sean would be digging their way under the compound fence.

Sure enough, through the gloom and driving rain he was able to make out the two figures digging pebbles from under the electrified fence. Within a few minutes he was able to see them both wriggle under the fence and make their way across the compound, melting into the night and the driving rain.

****

Inside the compound the two, balaclaved figures took shelter behind the two humming transformers. The noise the transformers made was quite deafening close up. The driving rain caused them to hum and sputter even more than usual.

The Irishman set about fixing the first charge into position, whilst his assistant sorted out the various bits of ancillary equipment. Satisfied with the charge on the first transformer, the two men moved positions to the second one. As they were busy setting the second charge in place they both paused. A very different sound from the noise of the transformers could be heard in the distance.

'Helicopter?' whispered the Irishman.

Both men looked at each other briefly, exchanging questioning glances. Then there came the sound of raised voices from the direction of the bird hide at Energy Heights. Suddenly it was bathed in light as the approaching helicopter climbed above the trees and shined its powerful search light beam on the area.

'Hell Fire! It's a trap!' Exclaimed Sean, immediately realizing what was happening. Without another word he turned and bolted for the hole that they had excavated earlier, under the compound fence. Behind him his accomplice was a little slower off the mark, but also dropped everything and made a beeline for the same point.

They were both aware that the helicopter could come no closer because of the dangers of overhead power lines.

This meant they could run across the substation compound in relative darkness. The Irishman reached the fence first, wriggled under it and was up and running on the far side, before his accomplice had arrived.

'Wait for me Sean' He shouted 'Give us a hand under the wire'

The Irishman stopped briefly and turned. 'Not a hope pal. It's every man for himself now.'

With that he turned and continued his dash towards Knackers Hole, leaving his partner to make his own way under the compound fence.

****

From his position overlooking the compound Ben could hear the sound of the helicopter as it approached.

'What's a helicopter doing out at this time of night.' He thought to himself. 'The Grid don't normally check the wires at night.'

Then as the helicopter climbed over the trees and shone its light on the bird hide, he realized that it must be the police. All hell then broke loose. He could see a figure caught in the powerful beam of the helicopter search-light, running down the hill away from the bird hide. There came the sound of a large dog barking and then three policemen burst into view, closing in on him. As they grabbed him by various parts of his body, Ben could hear him protesting loudly. It was Ian, the university man, who had so nearly discovered him in Canterbury Woods.

'Get off me you fascist pigs. Touch me and I'll have my lawyer onto you.' He shouted, as they wrestled him to the floor.

They pushed him face down in the long grass, pushing his arms together behind his back, as one of the officers placed handcuffs around his wrists.

Then they lifted him to a standing position as he continued to struggle and protest. 'If you've got grass stains on these Armani jeans I'm going to sue you, you bloody flatfoots.'

Then Ben was able to make out two female police officers escorting a woman down the slope from the bird hide. She was offering no obvious resistance, her head held up in a defiant pose as she was guided down to where her partner was still creating such a rumpus. It was Erica Butler.

'Give it a rest Ian.' She commanded of her accomplice. 'OK which one of you is in charge? I expect to be able to make a telephone call to my solicitor immediately and we are not saying anything until we do.' She spoke in clear commanding tones.

Perhaps a minute had passed since the helicopter first appeared. Then it occurred to Ben that the police had only been focusing on the bird hide and not the electricity compound. He wondered what was going on down there.

Where had the police come from so quickly? Surely Paddy couldn't have raised the alarm so soon? It then struck Ben that the whole thing must have been a set-up. They must have known about the plot all along. But why were there no police arresting the two in the compound?

Then in the half-light cast by the searchlight of the hovering helicopter, he caught sight of one of the men inside the compound. The hooded figure approached the compound fence just below where Ben was crouched in the undergrowth. Not wanting to be discovered by him Ben turned and scuttled deeper into the cover of Broad Oak Woods at the top of the slope.

****

Things were not quite going as Smith had planned. It was evident to him that the Irishman was about to get away into the darkness. No armed police were in place to intercept Kelly, so he, Smith of the Squad, was going to have to have his finest hour and tackle Kelly alone. He was sure Kelly would be armed, but he had to at least delay him for long enough for the police to sort things out. So in the best traditions of 'cops and robbers', he put his head down and sprinted after the shadowy figure now headed for the hole in the boundary fence and freedom.

****

Having cleared the compound fence Sean made his

way a little more stealthily towards the hole they had made in the outer perimeter fence, beyond the Pylon Bird sculpture. He felt confident of his escape; comforted by the hard metallic object he now carried clutched in his hand. The rest of them could look out for themselves he thought.

Then he heard a noise behind him. Assuming it to be his co-conspirator he slowed slightly and glanced briefly over his shoulder. He just had sufficient time to see a blurred balaclava clad figure coming at him. Next second he was falling through the air, his adversary holding tightly onto his legs in a classic rugby tackle.

His legs now locked together Sean went down heavily, but managed to roll, twist himself out of the grasp of his pursuer and acrobatically end up in a standing position facing his now prostrate adversary. In his hand he held the gun, which was now pointed directly at the man who had tripped him.

'Who the hell are you?' The Irishman spat the words out.

'Smith.' Was all his attacker said, as he climbed slowly to his feet.

He quickly grasped what had transpired, now aware that it had been a setup and that the man standing in front of him was responsible for his current predicament. He knew exactly what he would do next.

'Say goodbye copper.'

Chapter Twenty Three
A Bird in your Head
(is worth two in a bush)

Desperate to find out where the man he had seen in the electricity compound had gone to, Ben scuttled through Broad Oak Woods to the Valley of Death. Moving more carefully now he avoided the main 400Kv Path and scrambled up Oak Mound.

As he approached the southern end of the mound he heard voices coming from the direction of the Pylon Bird sculpture at Knackers Hole. As he peered into the gloom ahead he could pick out two figures, just beyond the dark silhouette of the sculpture. Standing facing in Ben's direction, with a black balaclava covering his head, was what Ben assumed to be one of the men. He had both his hands held high above his head, a pose that struck Ben as slightly comical at first. The humour of the situation quickly disappeared when Ben realized that the other figure, a black hooded top pulled over his head, was holding something in his right hand, it was a gun and he was pointing it directly at the other man.

Ben was now confused. Why were the two men not running? Surely they wanted to escape the police who were now swarming around the place? Why was the man nearest to him pointing a gun at his accomplice?

He was now close enough to hear the nearer of the two men shout in the familiar Irish accent, he had heard in the early hours of the morning at Hornbeam Horseshoe.

'Say goodbye copper'

****

Ben immediately realized that the man with the gun must be Sean and that the man he had called 'copper' must be one of the policemen involved in the trap. He must have been waiting in the undergrowth and intercepted Sean to prevent his escape.

'What happens next?' Thought Ben, in a state of confusion.

Then realizing that the gunman was likely to use his weapon on the policeman, Ben decided he had to have a go and do something.

Between him and the Irishman stood the gigantic Pylon Bird, looming some 5 metres above the pair. Ben moved slowly forward trying to get closer and hear more clearly what was being said, using the Pylon Bird to provide a little cover for his actions. The high winds and driving rain helped cover any noise he made as he picked his way through the long wet grass around the sculpture.

What was he to do to stop the policeman being shot? There was no way he could get near to the gunman and disarm him, even if he was strong enough to do so. Then he noticed that the Pylon Bird was leaning quite significantly. The high winds must have caused the giant bird's considerable mass to shift. He could see that the original stakes put in the ground by Peter the sculptor were actually inadequate for their purpose.

The base of the structure was about half a metre off the ground on his side. The whole structure, with its significant weight, was ready to topple. All that was holding it in place was one of the rope guy lines anchored to a piece of angle iron buried in the ground closest to him. Every time the wind blew another gust of driving rain against the sculpture, the part of the base nearest to him lifted several centimetres further off the ground, causing the guy line to tense and temporarily stop the whole structure from toppling over.

He decided to get a little closer so that he could better hear what they were saying. As he moved into the open he noticed the policeman holding his arms aloft, stiffen slightly. Had he heard him? If so surely the Irishman, standing closer to Ben, would hear him also. He suddenly felt fear grip him, as the hairs on the back of his neck started to rise.

****

As the two men stood facing each other, the gunman pointed his firearm directly at Smith's chest. He was under no illusions, as to the hopelessness of his position. The man in front of him definitely had the advantage.

The police had reacted quickly, with the assault on the substation thwarted and the rest of the gang rounded up. Only the two men planting explosives had escaped immediate detection. He also knew enough about the man in front of him to realize that he was a desperate killer. Doubtless he had grown increasingly bitter during his time in the Maze Prison and had no intention of going back there.

Sean's escape route across Knackers' Hole and through the gap in the wire fence had been clear. The only thing between him and escape had been Smith's rugby tackle.

'Well this is a pretty turn of events. There's only one solution to this problem my friend'. He hissed, the gun fixed directly on Smith's body.

'So this is it then?' Said Smith, looking steadily into his adversary's eyes.

Then a slight movement beyond the Pylon Bird caught his eye and his body stiffened slightly as he watched the figure of the young boy stalking beyond the sculpture.

'What's he doing here?' He thought to himself. Was it possible that perhaps Ben had guessed what was going on and was somehow looking to help?

As the wind gusted again his eyes caught another movement, this time overhead, behind the Irishman. Without moving his head Smith lifted his eyes upwards towards the pointed beak of the Pylon Bird. He knew the man with the gun could not see his eyes in the poor light.

Then he realized what the boy was up to. The Pylon Bird was leaning towards them both. The only thing preventing it falling was the guy-line that the boy was now approaching.

Amazed at the nerve that the young if rather foolish lad was showing, he did a quick calculation and realized that Sean was standing slightly to one side of the leaning sculpture. Even if it toppled it would not strike him. Could he do anything to cause the other man to move to his left and directly under the bird?

'What next then copper' hissed the Irish accent as the two men anticipated the obvious end to the evening's proceedings.

'Copper?' He questioned, slipping into the Ulster accent he had learned whilst at University in Belfast. 'Now what would be making you think that I'm a copper then Michael? The police are not the only ones who want you stopped, you know'

Sean was immediately puzzled by this apparent stranger, who appeared to know his real name and who spoke to him with a Belfast accent and in such a familiar way.

'Who the hell are you then?' He questioned.

Seeing his opportunity Smith took a step forward and slightly to his right, his hands still raised above his head.

'Well Michael wouldn't you like to know?' He said.

The Irishman immediately responded by jerking the gun up towards his head, whilst taking a step backwards and to his left. 'Get back, unless you have some sort of death wish' he commanded.

The gunman had taken the bait. Aware that there was a limit to how far he could push his luck; Smith stopped and took a step backwards, but also to his right. He had hoped that his little ruse would sow a few seeds of doubt in the others mind and buy just a little more time.

'Haven't you ever wondered who put the finger on you and had you put away Mick? The only trouble with you being let out of the Maze was that you were a potential embarrassment to the organization. So we arranged for this little escapade. It worked a treat. Now the cops can put you back inside again'

Michael Kelly, alias Sean, was incredulous. 'You're talking rubbish, whoever you are.' But the doubt had been planted and Sean was desperate to know more about the man in front of him.

'First of all you can take that thing off your head. I want to see your eyes before I shoot yer'. As he spoke he took a step forward.

****

Terrified, Ben had frozen when he saw the balaclavad man stiffen. Then as the man moved forward and the Irishman took a step back, he heard muffled commands and realized that if he couldn't hear them, then no-one was going to hear any noise he made either.

The two figures in front of him continued to gesticulate at each other, obviously carrying on some sort of discussion that he was not privy to, thanks to the driving wind and rain.

It was then that he realized what the man in the balaclava had been trying to do. He had cleverly managed to maneuver the Irishman directly under the leaning Pylon Bird.

Ben knew exactly what he had to do. Moving carefully he took 10 paces towards the guy rope, which was now slack as the wind died down. All he had to do was undo the knot on the rope and the whole sculpture would fall. As he fumbled with the wet rope he realized that the knot was far too tight. What was he to do?

Suddenly another gust of wind whistled through the trees. The Pylon Bird lurched forward, its wooden structure groaning under the strain.

As the wind strained against the towering structure, the Irishman turned towards the noise and caught sight of Ben. The gun in his hand moved in his direction and Ben suddenly realized he was going to shoot him and there was nothing he could do about it! He fleetingly wondered what it would feel like, to be shot.

As Sean turned, the man in the black balaclava saw his chance and rushed at the Irishman whilst he was momentarily distracted. But Sean was no slouch. He took a step away from the onrushing figure, adjusted the movement of his gun and squeezed the trigger.

As the gun went off, the onrushing figure landed in a heap on the floor.

****

To Ben everything seemed to be happening so fast. He heard a shot, but realized it had not been fired at him. He saw the body of the onrushing man twist in mid air and guessed he must have taken the bullet that was meant for Ben. As Sean took a step towards the prone figure lying in the grass he assumed he was preparing to finish the job.

It was then that Ben caught site of the gleaming metal in the long grass. He guessed that it must be Peter's missing knife. He knew exactly what he had to do next. Grabbing hold of the knife he picked it up and ran its superbly sharp blade across the now taught guy rope. He just hoped the blade was as sharp as Peter claimed it was.

As he drew the 10-centimetre blade across the rope it bit deep into the twisted strands. Almost in slow motion Ben saw the strands separate and then the rope part with a crack.

With nothing to hold it back, the weight of the sculpture toppled forward.

As the man with the gun stepped forward towards the prostrate body in front of him, he detected a movement in the corner of his eye. As he twisted his head round all he could see was a giant red beak driving down at him.

With the power of the wind and the momentum of the bird's long neck driving it downward, the bird's sharp wooden beak was driven hard into his skull. He immediately dropped to the ground on top of the prostrate body before him, taking the full weight of the rest of the sculpture as it toppled.

As Ben stood watching the scene before him he wondered if he had killed the Irishman. Neither of the men moved. Ben moved slowly forward. Both men seemed lifeless, but Ben decided he'd better pick up the gun anyway.

Thinking that he had probably succeeded in knocking out the Irishman, Ben wondered who the other man was. Assuming him to be a policeman he took a step closer to see if he was OK. Just then he started to move. He wasn't dead after-all. Ben breathed a sigh of relief.

So who was this mystery man?

Then it occurred to him that one other member of the gang was as yet unaccounted for. One who had been in the compound with the Irishman. What had become of that scheming toad Alan?

Then as if to confirm Ben's worst fears the stranger tugged the balaclava off his head to reveal an olive skinned face topped by greasy black hair and an all too familiar and unsmiling face. Alan!

Ben had knocked out or killed the Irishman, only to spare the life of the other saboteur. But why had Sean been trying to shoot his co-saboteur? It didn't make sense. Totally confused by events Ben just panicked.

As Alan staggered to his feet holding his blood soaked head Ben instinctively turned and ran, the gun still in his hand. His legs pumping as hard as they could he tried to put as much distance between himself and the events of Knackers' Hole. As the steps next to Marsh Orchid Mere appeared before him, Ben took them two at a time, his heart pounding, his lungs bursting and his thoughts racing. As he topped the steps his path was barred by a dark dog-shaped shadow.

Ben just froze as a low growl erupted from the dog as it barred its teeth at him. Then a familiar whistle rang through the air and the dog was gone.

'Now what have we here' Came an unfamiliar voice from the darkness of the trees. As the bulky figure stepped out into the path in front of him, a powerful torch beam was directed straight into Ben's eyes. 'Are you a saboteur as well?' Enquired the voice.

'No I'm Ben,' He answered shakily.

'Then why are you carrying a sidearm young fella?'

Came the voice from behind the torchlight. As the torchlight was directed away from Ben's eyes, he immediately noticed that the man was wearing a pair of dark tinted glasses, despite it being nighttime.

Just then the dog returned, mercifully for Ben on a leash, accompanied by its handler. Even in the poor light Ben was able to recognize the dog and its handler, as the pair he and Lizzie had observed on the reserve several weeks earlier.

'All sorted back here' Said the policeman. 'Where's the Irishman?'

'Perhaps this young man can throw some light on the matter, since he doesn't look like the kind of villain who normally carries a gun with him on a dark night out' Mused the man in the dark glasses.

'There are two more behind me.' Blubbed Ben, as he held out the gun for the man to take it from him. He had no idea what was going on but suddenly felt mightily relieved at the sight of the policeman and his dog.

'OK, Lambert. I suggest you and the dog go and investigate.'

As the dog and its handler ran past Ben and down the steps in the direction of the carnage meated out by the now fallen Pylon Bird, Ben felt a little more confident.

'Who are you?' He asked of the stranger.

'Let's just call me Cyclops shall we?' He answered.

Taking the gun and slipping it into his coat pocket, Cyclops took Ben by the sleeve and guided him back towards the steps. 'Come on young man. Let's see what you've been up to shall we?'

As they approached Knackers' Hole, Ben was able to make out some activity in the beam of the torch carried by Cyclops. The policeman was now pulling a handcuffed figure to his feet, as his Alsatian sat obediently by, releasing a low growl at the man being manhandled to his feet.

Then, as the two men came closer, Ben finally got a clear look at the handcuffed man. When he saw him, it was like a bolt out of the blue. It was Peter. 'But that's Peter, Peter the sculptor. I think there must have been a mistake. Paddy went to fetch Peter about twenty minutes ago. I guess it wasn't him that called the police and tell you to come down here?'

As if reading his thoughts Cyclops said 'We've been expecting this for some time now. We've been waiting for Mr. Kelly here to make his move. I'm afraid he's not your friend Peter the sculptor, although it was one of the skills he picked up during his time in the Maze Prison in Belfast. No this is Michael Kelly, alias Sean O'Reilly, alias Peter the Sculptor. He was one of the IRA prisoners released last year, but now he's going back to where he belongs'

Ben looked wide-eyed at Peter.

'Well a fine friend you turned out to be, young un' he said. 'You're quite the detective aren't yi? It was nice knowing you, but it looks as though I'll be honing mi artistic skills for a little longer at 'Her Majesty's Pleasure'. Just like art, not everything is quite as it may appear.' Said Peter.

'But what about the money you promised my dad to save the nature reserve?' Gasped Ben. 'He was counting on that to keep it open'.

'Sorry kiddo. Guess no-ones a winner tonight are they?'

'Take him down to the station Lambert, with the rest of the gang.' Said Cyclops, signaling in the direction of the car park.

'So, who's a clever little chap?' Came an all too familiar voice behind him.

Chapter Twenty Four
Smith Shares his Secret

As Ben turned he was alarmed to see the blood soaked face of Alan looking at him with those piercing, unsmiling eyes of his.

'But he's one of them also' Ben said to Cyclops. 'I heard you plotting with your friends at the Roundhouse'

'Did you now?' Enquired Alan. 'You are a busy-little-body aren't you? I'll lay odds it was you and not that pheasant that was lurking in the nettles all the while.'

'And we saw you with Scarface sneaking round the substation one Sunday morning. What were you up to if you were not up to mischief?'

'Blimey!' Whistled Alan 'You get everywhere!'

'Looks to me as though you have not been as careful as you should have been Agent Smith' Laughed Cyclops 'I think it might be time to pension you off. I think we've already found your replacement'

Then Ben witnessed something totally unexpected. A trace of a smile played across Alan's face. The smile grew into a grin and then the grin turned into a laugh. Soon both Cyclops and Smith were in full flow, as tears came to their eyes.

Then both men straightened their faces as Cyclops spoke softly. 'I'm going to have to ask you not to mention Agent Smith or myself to anyone else young man, at least not until we have caught and convicted the rest of the animal activist cell. Do you think you could do that for us?'

'Yes I suppose so' said Ben, thinking how much he really wanted to tell Paddy and Lizzie about the night's events.

'We're going to have to explain what happened to the Pylon Bird ' said Smith 'I suppose we could blame vandals or something, since the real reason for it's destruction can't be revealed. Anyway, thanks for saving my life young man. You've got a hell of a lot of bottle for a young un.' And he shook Ben's hand in gratitude, although Ben still found it hard not to stiffen at his touch.

'Good now that we've got all that sorted out, you'd best be getting off to the hospital Agent Smith' said Cyclops 'Whilst I get this young man back to his parents. I'm sure they'll be worried about you'.

'Gosh, I'd forgotten about them. Paddy was supposed to fetch them if he couldn't get Peter' said Ben.

'See you Ben' said Smith as he slipped through the hole in the nature reserve fence.

'Bye.' Replied the still reeling Ben, as he gave a weak wave to the receding figure.

Smith then walked a little way down the road to his waiting motorbike on the forecourt of the Forge Bike Shop, where he had left it several hours earlier.

'The nurses are going to tell me off for riding without a crash helmet I guess. At least I've got a good alibi to explain the blood' He chuckled to himself.

Just then a grey Ford Focus estate, driven by Ben's grim-faced dad, drove past as it approached the front gates of the nature reserve. On the back seat a young French boy looked agog at the man climbing onto the motorcycle.

'It is him!' shouted Paddy.

'Who?' Said Dad.

'That man Alan' Replied Paddy.

'Well I'm sure if he's as bad as you say, then the police will pick him up. It looks to me as though the place is crawling with them.'

Once he'd parked the car, Dad went off to find out what was going on. There must have been a dozen or more policemen, dogs and vehicles in the car park by now.

Paddy climbed out of the car and walked straight into Peter.

'Peter, you are here? I called at your house but you not there' Said the young French boy. Peter said nothing. Then Paddy noticed that he had his hands behind his back and was being marched away to a waiting police car.

'Paddy!' Shouted Ben

Paddy turned in the direction of the caller. 'Aah Ben, what is happening? Why is Peter take away by Policeman?'

'He's one of them.' Said Ben 'I'll explain it all later'.

Chapter Twenty Five
The Final Twist

The police activity around Canterbury continued into the early hours of the morning. A number of raids were made on addresses around the city, where the occupants were rounded up by armed policemen, with numerous computers and bags of paper being removed as evidence.

Up at the university the research laboratory lights suddenly went out, at a prearranged time. This was the signal for a small band of black clad figures to cut their way through the perimeter fence and head towards the primate section. Thirty second's later the lights came back on to reveal a cordon of heavily armed police officers. The group was arrested without so much as a struggle.

By the following morning several mobile television units descended upon Canterbury with reporters shooting footage of the laboratories and the substation. No mention was made of the nature reserve or the son of its manager. The police had agreed to keep Ben's name and involvement concealed from public attention.

Ben's mum and dad had been alarmed by the scale of the activity and the potential risk to Ben. He received a few sharp words about taking risks, but this was quickly forgotten with the relief that came from knowing that he was safe. Ben had to go round to Paddy's house and apologize to his mum for getting him involved.

Within a few days the press and TV attention quickly evaporated and life on the reserve could return to normal. Then a week later, whilst Ben was playing down at the nature reserve, three cars pulled into the car park. Three of the four occupants of the cars were dressed in dark suits. One of them looked particularly familiar to Ben, he wore a pair of dark glasses. The forth visitor was dressed in a police uniform, but wore a peaked hat instead of a policeman's helmet. Ben guessed he was a pretty senior officer.

Dad met them out by the Water Cycle, which provided an opportunity for brief discussion, before he ushered them into his office.

****

The four visitors squeezed together into Dad's cramped office exchanging pleasantries as tea and coffee was served. Ben waited outside in the main office wondering what was going on, when a further car pulled into the car park and a familiar figure walked purposefully towards the reserve offices. Without so much as a flicker of recognition in Ben's direction, Creamer burst into Dad's office.

'Franklin.' He said, hardly even noticing the four visitors. 'Could I speak to you alone for a minute?'

'Certainly Mr. Creamer' His Dad replied, looking a little nonplussed by Creamer's abrupt manner. 'Please excuse me for a minute gentlemen.'

Dad stepped out of the office, leaving the door ajar and stood facing Creamer, whose arms were folded in front of him. He had a triumphant look on his face.

'I'll come to the point.' Said Creamer. 'The committee has decided that since your promised financial support from the Environment Trust has not been forthcoming, you have therefore failed to balance your budget. Failure to achieve this target, as explained to you earlier in the year, means the nature reserve will be closed by the start of January.'

Dad looked totally crestfallen, although he had been expecting something like this ever since it turned out that Peter's promised funding had been as false as his identity.

'I'm sorry to hear the news, but could you please tell me why you have been so intent to see us fail Mr. Creamer?' Said Dad, looking Creamer directly in the eye.

'Contrary to what you may think, it is nothing personal.' Said Creamer, looking a little awkward. 'The nature reserve has proved that it cannot support itself financially and so the Committee has decided that it should close. That's all. Now I must be going.' Said Creamer and turned to depart.

'Just a minute Mr. Creamer.' Came a voice from behind the dark glasses. 'Can I introduce you to Peter Jones - The Chief Constable for Kent, Stephen Johnson –

Vice Chairman of The Grid and Alex Jennison – Director of the Canterbury Wildlife Trust.'

Creamer visibly rocked on his heels as he took in the gathered officials he had so rudely disturbed a few seconds earlier. 'Sorry gentlemen, I'm afraid Mr. Franklin failed to notify me of your visit.'

'That's because no one knew we were coming.' Said Alex Jennison. 'I have heard about you from a number of sources, but I hadn't realized how rude you actually are!'

'I was aware of the threat to the reserves future, but do I understand from your remarks that the nature reserve is actually to be closed down?' Asked Stephen Johnson. 'I am very disappointed not to have been notified of your decision directly. I would have thought that as one of the partners involved in supporting the nature reserve, we would have been consulted regarding its fate.'

'Well, of course' Stammered Creamer. 'I was going to notify you immediately, but the decision was only made one hour ago'

'And you saw fit to drive down here personally to bring the glad tidings?' Added the Chief Constable. 'How thoughtful.'

Creamer just stared at the four men seated in Dad's office. Ben, who had been privy to the whole episode also stood speechless but listening to every word. His initial feelings had been of sadness when Creamer had first announced the reserve's closure. Now he was starting to feel a little better as he watched Creamer wriggle in front of his dad's guests.

'You may not be aware of what transpired over the last few weeks at this substation?' Continued the Chief Constable. 'This was the site of a very high profile security operation involving terrorists.'

'Yes of course I knew that' Creamer replied, his face now almost white.

At this point the man in dark glasses stood up and pointed towards Ben, standing in the corner of the main office behind Creamer. 'What you won't know is the vital role played by this young man. Without his timely intervention the whole operation might have foundered and certainly one of my men would be in a coffin at this moment in time. It is thanks to him, his father and the nature reserve that the operation was the success it turned out to be.'

'Well I'm sure that's very good' Said Creamer, recovering his composure a little. 'But that is not a matter for the Committee. All we are interested in is making sure that rate-payers' money is not wasted.'

'Well in that case Mr. Creamer I don't think we should waste any more of your valuable time' Said Mr. Johnson. 'Doubtless you are keen to be getting back to your office to provide rate-payers with value for money. However can I just share with you what I was about to share with Mr. Franklin when you so rudely burst in? The Grid is extremely grateful to Ben and Mr. Franklin. Perhaps a little belatedly, we now realize that retaining a busy nature reserve on site, not only improves the security of the substation, but also offers excellent public relations benefits for the company.'

Ben wondered where this speech was leading to, but he was delighted by Mr. Johnson's next statement.

'The Grid has decided to end its partnership with your Committee and start a new partnership with Mr. Jennison's Canterbury Wildlife Trust.'

Alex Jennison then took his turn. 'Since Mr. Franklin and his staff will no longer be employed by you, they will be offered new jobs with the Wildlife Trust, thanks to the financial support promised by The Grid.'

'Wow' Said Ben 'That's great news!'

'You can go now Mr. Creamer' Said Dad. 'I look forward to receiving formal notification of my redundancy at your earliest opportunity. Goodbye.'

Creamer just stared at Dad and the assembled officials.

'I'm sorry Mr. Creamer, but I have some important business to attend to and I am afraid it is confidential. Goodbye Mr. Creamer.' Said Dad.

Without another word, Creamer had to leave the reserve for the second time in recent weeks, with his tail tucked firmly between his legs, a defeated man.

'Come here Ben' Said Cyclops. 'There are a number of gentlemen here who would like to speak to you.'

Dad then marshaled Ben into his office to shake hands with the gathered dignitaries, each of whom stood respectfully as he was introduced to them.

This was a day to remember.

****

Next day Ben was standing with his Dad, Lizzie, Paddy, Paddy's sister Valentine and his mother, on the platform at Canterbury West Station. Paddy was due back at School in Nice, his holiday in England now over.

'Sorry to see you all going.' Said Dad to the whole Davidson family.

'Yes parting is such sweet sorrow' Said Mrs. Davidson, 'But I hope we might see you in Nice next summer. You are all invited'

'Really?' said Ben. 'Can we go Dad?'

'I don't see why not. That's very generous of you Astrid.' He said turning to Mrs. Davidson.

'Not at all. It will be our pleasure won't it Patrick? Or should I call you Paddy now?' She said to Paddy, with an impish smile on her face.

'Non Maman, Paddy is my English name, when I am playing with my good friends Ben and Lizzie. In France I will be Patrick.' Said Paddy to his mother. 'Now I must say goodbye to my friends'

He then turned to Ben. 'Goodbye Ben, it has been a wonderful holiday and my English is now much better thank you. Father will be very pleased with me and it's all because of you'

Ben put out his hand to shake hands with his good friend, but Paddy ignored it, taking Ben's shoulders in his hands he proceeded to kiss Ben on each cheek, much to Ben's acute embarrassment.

'You should get used to the French way if you are going to visit us next summer. Everyone kisses each other in France you know?' He said with a wink. Everyone laughed at this.

Nonetheless everyone exchanged goodbyes in the French way as the Ashford train pulled in.

Ben was sad to see his good friend leaving, but happy about the prospect of visiting Nice next summer.

'Don't forget to write!' Said Ben to the waving Paddy as the train pulled out of the station. As Mrs. Davidson had said, parting was such sweet sorrow.

Chapter Twenty Six
The Largest Pike in British Inland Waters

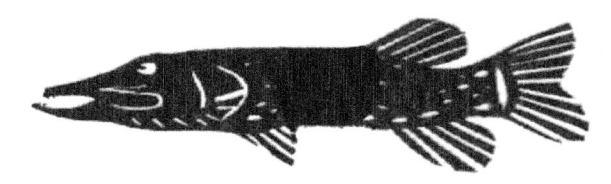

After seeing Paddy off from the station, Dad returned them to the nature reserve. Lizzie had to go off for one of her riding, piano, dancing or other lessons, leaving Ben alone to think about events.

Feeling a little saddened by the loss of his good friend Paddy, he decided to get Conker out and go for a quiet cruise on the lake. Equipped with life jacket, electric outboard and his cell phone, he gave a twist on the tiller and headed out into the nearest lake - Gittchee Gummee. Instead of heading north towards Barton Broad, he decided to head south and pass through the Reed Curtain and beyond into Damselfly Lake.

He always liked taking this route, which required him to get the electric motor up to full power and then burst through the Reed Curtain into the lake beyond. The reeds resisted the forward motion of the boat, which almost ground to a halt due to the dragging stems. As Conker cleared the reeds, the outboard picked up speed and Ben felt the thrill as the boat gunned into Damselfly Lake. In the distance Ben could just make out the upturned hull of the Damselfly, a predecessor of Conker, which had sunk in the middle of the lake. The wreck was often a good place to view fish in the clear water of the lake.

However, he was distracted by a pungent smell in the air, which increased in intensity as he approached Damselfly. Then in amongst the shorter reeds close to Alder Tree Jetty, Ben caught sight of a large floating mass in the water. It looked like some sort of body, floating in the water. Ben approached cautiously half expecting to find the bloated carcass of the Headless Dog.

This time he could see it was quite distinctly fishy in shape. What's more the smell was becoming quite disgusting. As he drew alongside the carcass, Ben killed the engine. He could now see that the body was that of an enormous pike floating on the lake surface. Its long thin face tapered into powerful jaws, revealing lines of deadly-looking, backward facing, sharp teeth. Ben recalled the fleeting glimpse of the monster that had taken his fishing rod, and very nearly him, with it into the depths of the lake.

This was a monster fish, probably some four feet in length. Grabbing hold of the fishes tail he heaved hard and pulled the beast into the boat, its head and tail stretching the full width of Conker. Ben wondered if this was the Monster of Broad Oak. Could it be the pike he had encountered before? It seemed a lot smaller out of water. He was about to start the outboard and take it back to show the others when he heard a voice behind him.

'Caught a big un have you?' It was Danny the poacher.

'It was floating in the reeds' Said Ben.

'I know' Agreed Danny 'I caught it two nights ago. Took me ages to land it. Biggest fish I've ever landed in over fifty years. I let it go, but the poor thing was old and spent - like me. It was as much as it could do to drag itself out as far as those reeds, to die. Now it's time for it to return to the lake, feeding all the little things as it rots.'

'It does stink a bit.' Said Ben. 'I was just going to show it to everyone else at the nature reserve office'

'No don't do that. Give it some dignity. It was king below the water when it was alive, but now it's just a smelly old carcass. Do me a favour would you young un?' Said Danny.

'OK' said Ben. 'What do you want me to do?'

'Take it back into the thicker reeds and chuck it overboard.' Pleaded Old Danny. 'I've been chasing the Monster of Broad Oak Lakes for longer than I care to remember. He's the spirit of the lake and his identity should remain a secret forever. Anyway if you show it off to the papers every angler for miles will be trying to catch more of them. You'll just be bringing more trouble upon the nature reserve.'

'But there may be more of them.' Said Ben.

'No' Replied Danny. 'No more. It takes a pike fifty years to reach that size. We've caught the Monster of the Lake. Let him be our secret. Put him back.

Guiding Conker into the denser reeds, Ben got as far into them as they would allow. Then putting both his hands around the massive shoulders of the fish he heaved it tail first into the reeds.

'Done it.' Shouted Ben.

'Good on yer young 'un. Time I packed in as well. Been fishing these lakes too long now. Can't get any better than that one. Reckon I've finally caught the Biggest Pike in British Inland Waters, so I reckon I'll do something different now. Perhaps I'll take up ballroom dancing,' He said with a wink at Ben. 'See you about kid'

As Ben watched Danny go he wondered about what Old Danny had said. Was this the Monster of Broad Oak Lakes? He could have sworn his fish was even bigger. Just then there came a loud thrashing sound from the water by the reeds, where he had just dumped the dead pike. Turning to see what the noise was he could see nothing.

'Monsters.' Laughed Ben. 'I wonder if they have them in Nice?'

Then sitting on the stern seat of Conker, he gave the tiller a twist, causing Conker to jerk forward, carrying Ben back to the nature reserve buildings.

****

In the dark waters below, the owner of a pair of dark malevolent eyes watched the boy in the boat move silently away. It had seen the boy before and still bore the hook in its mouth, from their earlier encounter.

The Largest Pike in British Inland Waters.

The End.

Broad Oak Lakes Nature Reserve - Canterbury

Printed in Great Britain
by Amazon